AWAKE

AWAKE

A Memoir

Jen Hatmaker

BLUEBIRD

First published 2025 by Avid Readers Press
An Imprint of Simon & Schuster, LLC

First published in the UK 2025 by Bluebird
an imprint of Pan Macmillan
The Smithson, 6 Briset Street, London ECIM 5NR
EU representative: Macmillan Publishers Ireland Ltd, 1st Floor,
The Liffey Trust Centre, 117–126 Sheriff Street Upper,
Dublin 1 D01 YC43
Associated companies throughout the world

HB ISBN 978-1-0350-8192-9
TPB ISBN 978-1-0350-8193-6

1 3 5 7 9 8 6 4 2

A CIP catalogue record for this book is available from the British Library.

Printed and bound by CPI Group (UK) Ltd, Croydon CRO 4YY

Visit **www.panmacmillan.com/bluebird** to read more about
all our books and to buy them.

This book is for my people who saw me through.

Your names are all in here.

You are the great loves of my life.

You are my forever.

Contents

Author's Note

To protect the privacy of individuals involved and streamline the chronology, some names, identifying details, and dates in this memoir have been altered while remaining true to the core experiences.

Also, it must be said that in any narrative, the story belongs to the storyteller. I am deeply aware that this is my story, my version, my experience. I am deciding what to include and exclude. Some choices I am making for the sake of someone else's privacy, as not everything is mine to tell, even though the partiality leaves a few holes in the story.

It is not only possible but certain that at some inflection point, someone else will say, "That's not how I remember that." Or "I have a different perspective." Childhood memories vary wildly from child to child, even inside the same family. One marriage, two people, two stories, or at least two nuanced versions.

I am also wary of defaulting to uncomplicated categories: the hero, the victim, the villain. My story in its starkest terms lends itself to those, and it is tempting to use them. You'd probably forgive me. "That makes sense," you would say. "Those are just the facts." And yes, they are, but the picture must be zoomed out to be, not accurate per se, but *more* accurate.

Alas, the memoirist's dilemma. I can only tell my version. It is what I know. It is what I remember. It is what I felt. Trying to include everyone's disparate versions would fragment this story beyond useful-ness and, for me, truth. So I am left with the uncomfortable task of calling it like I saw it, knowing no two people in this story would tell it the exact same way.

So, reader, the story you have here? Is mine.

my heart woke me crying last night
how can i help i begged
my heart said
write the book

—Rupi Kaur, *Milk and Honey*

part one

THE END

Over.

At 2:30 a.m. on July 11, 2020, out of a dead sleep, I hear five whispered words not meant for me: "I just can't quit you." My husband of twenty-six years is voice-texting his girlfriend next to me in our bed.

It is the end of my life as I know it.

The next four hours are chaos. While he eventually passes out from a treacherous combination of booze and exposure, I follow a trail of betrayal on his computer, an entire other life. My body is frozen. I can't even cry. My whole world is slipping away click by click. I float above myself watching my brain absorb the impossible, watching my heart splinter. So this is what it looks like when a life unravels in real time. It is quieter than I expected.

The kids are upstairs asleep, unaware that their story has just split in half. They went to bed in the hazy, lazy days of summer polluted by a four-month-old COVID outbreak but otherwise sleeping the comfortable sleep of kids whose parents will always be just downstairs; family disruption might come from outside but never from within. Not ours anyway. I keep thinking: "They don't know. I don't want to know. I want to go upstairs with them and not know."

At 6:30 a.m., having endured as much discovery as a soul can take in four middle-of-the-night hours, I wake him up and ask for the full truth and nothing less. He is unwilling. I tell him to pack his shit and get out.

It is the last night he ever spends at our house.

I text my parents and sisters and brother: I need you at Mom's house right now. No one asks for an explanation. This type of summons signals a crisis, and everyone is there by 7:00 a.m. I pull into their driveway and Mom is waiting outside. She has no idea what has happened, but she opens her arms with tears streaming and I finally collapse. I scream like a wounded animal. I can't stop. I've lost all sense of time and space. I feel my siblings throw their arms around me, but I am gone.

Dead Rose

I am a high school freshman attending the first session of True Love Waits at my church. This course, the leaders tell our parents, will teach us teenagers about purity and how to stave off our burgeoning sexuality. There is nothing more precious than (a girl's) virginity, so the deacons and their wives would discuss the perils of heavy petting and spaghetti straps; they'd been trained on the curriculum.

Before they separate the guys and girls into Sunday school classrooms, the student pastor walks to the front of the dingy youth room holding a fresh red rose: "Isn't this flower beautiful, everyone?" We all agree that it is. So far, we are nailing our coursework. "Girls, right now, you are like this lovely rose. The most beautiful possible gift." I wonder why only the girls resemble the flower. I wonder who we are a gift for.

"This"—he holds out the blooming rose—"is like presenting yourself *pure* to your husband on your wedding night. Perfect and preserved! But when you start giving your body to your little boyfriends, you begin destroying the gift." At this alarming statement, he plucks the petals off the rose one at a time and lets them fall to the stained carpet:

"You let him touch your body." Pluck.

"You take off your clothes." Pluck.

"You engage in inappropriate acts." Pluck.

"You have sexual intercourse." Pluck.

We are frozen in our metal folding chairs. I have barely even kissed

5

a boy. I feel wildly embarrassed but can't figure out why. All of a sudden, I am hyperaware of my body and burning with shame; did that first kiss with Gary Whipple in seventh grade cost me a petal?? I glance nervously at the other girls, wondering if they knew we were such a problem. This was news to me. I can't look at the boys. I think maybe my Forenza shirt is too tight? It felt fine ten minutes ago. My cheeks are flushed with humiliation.

" . . . until all you have to offer your husband on your wedding night is this . . . " At this point the pastor holds up the barren, dead stick plucked of its petals, a pauper's gift if I ever saw one.

This is as confusing as it is denigrating. According to the indictment, didn't boys pluck those petals off? Were they also some sort of flower gradually losing their bloom? Or is sexual purity just the girls' responsibility and requirement? I scan the room with insider knowledge of high school behavior; some petals here have definitely been plucked, and frankly, I'd like to lose a few if I'm being honest. But apparently there is no coming back from being a slutty, stripped rose. Good luck finding a man who wants to marry a ruined stick.

At the onset of adolescent sexuality, I hear:

Girls' bodies are a problem and need to be heavily policed.

Girls' bodies are an offering for boys.

Girls' bodies are easily ruined.

Girls are responsible for a pure bedroom.

So our sexual deviance was our fault, and the boys' sexual deviance was our fault.

Got it.

Budget

It is July 1993. I am not yet nineteen, and my boyfriend and I are sitting across from my parents at their kitchen table explaining in reasonable terms why we should get married in December as a college sophomore and senior. We slide over a few numbers on a yellow legal pad and make our case:

"Between my job at the YMCA and his at the Western Outfitters, we will make almost $800 a month. That is more than enough to cover all our bills."

"Here is our budget. I think you'll find it extremely thorough."

"We one hundred percent plan to finish college. We will actually study *more* by living together."

Miraculously, my parents don't laugh. They look at our accounting and pretend to take it seriously. We will earn under $11,000 in a calendar year. We are playing at adulthood with as much earnestness as Baby Jesus in the manger. We have the trump card of my parents' story: They got married at twenty and twenty-four, so they have no leg to stand on.

We are wildly in love. We have dated a whopping ten months. Although I gave up a few petals, we are committed to (renewed) celibacy until December. We will get married in the godly-ish order so we can shag with impunity. This, we are told, is the right thing to do. It doesn't occur to us to just date, or be free young kids, or live together, or grow up, or discover who we are, or get more than two years away from prom before matrimony. We are in a conservative Baptist bubble where half the student body gets married before graduation. Being a teenage bride doesn't even seem weird.

My parents acquiesce. They say later I would have done what I wanted, so why make it harder? I can't remember *any adult* suggesting a college sophomore was perhaps not emotionally or mentally or relationally ready to be a wife. No one urged me to just be young, to live and grow and experience the world. I don't recall a shocked face, a suspicious response, a cautious warning. The community that raised me placed little premium on healthy young evolution.

He is going to be a student pastor and I am going to be a teacher and we are eager to sacrifice young adulthood for marriage.

We couldn't be happier.

Even then, even as a literal teenager, my hopes for the future are as deep as the ocean. We are in love, obsessed with each other. We plan to build a beautiful life. We will be faithful and serve God and be shining, twinkling lights in this dark world. He will be the leader of our family and I will be the best wing woman ever.

We write love letters and make homemade cards and give care packages and make out in our cars. We two-step at the Tumbleweed in Stillwater. We stay on the phone until 4:00 a.m. and dream about our future. We practice being youth pastors at a tiny local church where I am the students' actual peer. Our love: bottomless. Our devotion: incorruptible. Our loyalty: unquestionable.

I see the road ahead, and it is full of mutual adoration and meaningful ministry, tiny blond babies and a sweet little house. We will love our students and host Bunco with our neighbors. He will keep a meticulous yard, and I will wallpaper our dining room up to the chair rail. I will learn to cook like my grandma and use fresh garlic. We will build a family and a ministry and a whole life. One day we will walk our children down the aisle and rock our grandbabies on the porch. We will be lifers like both our parents. I will try so hard. We both will.

I am nineteen. He is twenty-one. On December 30, 1993, we hand over the keys to young adulthood and walk down the same church aisle my parents did. I am not old enough to drink at my reception.

Mrs. Anderson

I am a sixth grader, the worst time to be a human person in the span of a life. My body is hopeless, I cannot crack the hair code, Mom won't let me pierce my ears, everything feels rigged. I want to speak the language of the popular, but I am too awkward, too cerebral. I don't understand their dialect.

I am stunned at my classmates' natural charm. Notably, I study the way Laura Morgan walks and practice it in my full-length mirror; it involves curling your right fingers gently into your palm and slightly bending back your wrist. I don't understand this particular mannerism but its effect on me is undeniable. Plus, Laura is Catholic, which adds to her mystique. Her whole walking operation involves a casual gait while the posed right hand does a very specific *sashay*. It is a complicated endeavor, and I work on it, essentially, around the clock. Every Monday morning, I decide to debut my new walk at Mulberry School but I lose my nerve on the bus.

Through some twist of luck, this is the year I discover I am a little funny. Humor is my dad's native tongue, so I guess I absorbed it by proximity. This small emerging superpower is all I have. Style, money, looks, charisma—none, none, none, none. I can't do Laura's walk. We don't have cable, so I don't know the right shows. Mom refuses to buy me Guess jeans. My plastic glasses are a genuine tragedy. I have no other assets. But I learn to inject witty responses into the sixth-grade zeitgeist, and shockingly, astonishingly, the other kids laugh.

Unfamiliar with the concept of restraint, I put my new currency into high rotation. I stay hypervigilant for opportunities to demonstrate my comedy prowess. I find the middle of class an optimal time; I am hoping to impress Mrs. Anderson too. All I have ever been is smart and quiet. Being funny is fun. I haven't had many friends really, well, ever. The approval of my classmates is a stunning turn of events. My social anxiety begins fraying at the edges; a minuscule kernel of confidence takes root. My parents notice the change. They tell me later they are relieved. They'd wiped my many, many tears of loneliness.

I am at recess when a group of Cute Girls walks toward me in tandem:

"Jennifer, you'll never believe what Mrs. Anderson just said to us."

I mine my brain for a sharp witticism; a teacher deep cut always plays well.

"She pulled us all together in the hallway and asked why we even wanted to be friends with you! She said you were—what was the word she used, you guys? *Domineering*. She kept going on and on. She was really mean about it."

I am paralyzed. I stand there mute. My system is overloaded with shock.

Mrs. Anderson thinks badly of me? She finds me domineering? She doesn't know why anyone likes me? She is talking ugly about me to my new friends? I cannot get any of it to make sense. In eight seconds, I am handed a new story about myself, a thought I had never considered once:

I am too much.

I ache with humiliation and sorrow. For a few seconds, I try to pretend this doesn't bother me, but I start sobbing and run to the nurse's office. I lay on the sick cot and cover my head with a blanket. I am inconsolable. She has to call my parents. I am eleven.

Addendum: Dad

Let me explain something to you about Larry King, dad of Jen, Lindsay, Cortney, and Drew. In most ways, he will suffer a fool well past their merit. Not to put too fine a point on it, but I note the Haysville Police Department surrounding the house Dad rented to two "private dancers" who were six months behind in rent and apparently harboring a murderer. What I am saying is there were warning signs. Dad has a real bleeding heart in most cases, which makes him a disastrous landlord but a pretty good human.

There is one notable exception to his mercy: any offense to the aforementioned Jen, Lindsay, Cortney, and Drew.

There isn't enough ink in America to list the teachers, principals, coaches, club sponsors, deans, youth pastors, bosses, and arresting officers who found themselves on the wrong end of Larry King after some "unjust" treatment of his kids (scare quotes necessary in more than a few cases). Retribution was always swift. God's son Jesus as my witness, I am half a century old and Dad still offers to "make a call" on my behalf when something goes sideways.

All this to say, I don't want you thinking Mrs. Anderson didn't get her comeuppance. I can safely report Larry King made her regret talking shit about Jennifer King to those sixth-grade girls. If she thought *I* was too much, she hadn't yet seen my dad in action. The speed at which he raced our station wagon (the Gray Ghost) back to Mulberry

School to defend my case that day, while certainly criminal, was definitely heroic.

Domineering? We'll give you domineering, Mrs. Anderson. She probably never uttered that word again for the rest of her living days. Sure, we are Bible-believing folk and know God will eventually right every wrong, but while God is up there tarrying doing who knows what, Larry King will step in as his proxy. The King children don't have to wait for heaven's justice, and these are just the facts of the case, Your Honor.

Lawyer

It has been one day since I found out my life is not true, and I am sitting in an attorney's office. It is a Sunday but she goes to my church and agrees to meet me in her empty building. My mom and sisters are in the waiting room. They don't know how to help me outside of just being within touching range; I don't go anywhere without one or all of them for six solid weeks. Cortney is watching old *SNL* clips of Kristen Wiig because only absurd things make sense right now.

I have never been in a lawyer's office. It is cozy, like its only visitors are suing or defending or divorcing, and we can only manage these horrible things on soft couches. I float up to the ceiling and watch myself describing what I know so far, like telling the clinical story of someone else's fucked-up life. What I have already discovered suggests there will be no coming back. I am talking about divorcing my attorney's pastor, so we are both having an out-of-body experience. Later, I think to be grateful for her gentle face, her capacity to let me use ten thousand words when one hundred would have sufficed. I'd never said these things before. I am unpracticed at the story of desertion.

It is only much later I wonder: Why did I run straight to a lawyer in the first thirty-six hours? What instinct drove to an attorney instead of back to our marriage therapist? But I am not ready for this truth-telling yet. I was acting purely on intuition, which I only figured out later was the most trustworthy character in the play.

The Kids

At the genesis of this dreadful story, my oldest, Gavin, is a twenty-two-year-old recent graduate from Texas Tech. Sydney is a junior at the University of Texas. Caleb just graduated from high school. Ben is starting his junior year in high school, and Remy just finished eighth grade. Three of them live at home, and two are launched-ish. Three came from my body, and two through adoption, five beloved young Hatmakers.

They are teens and young adults, neither clueless nor naive. They have instant access to the chaos. There is no hiding a story when a dad goes to bed after a normal evening and moves out the next morning.

The family structure gives way immediately. Confrontations, shock, fury, grief. It is scorched earth. One hundred things shatter. His actions bulldoze a lifetime of instructional words and render them obsolete. Kids don't expect their parents to renege on the contract. If there is a breach, they assume it will be theirs as they test every limit and hedge the boundaries. Certainly not the parent, co-creator of the contract. We are all flayed by betrayal, not just me.

Reader, I will keep most of their story behind the firewall. It was all as painful as you think.

Jeremiah

The heart is deceitful above all things and beyond cure. Who can understand it?

—Jeremiah 17:9

I am taught this baseline at church from the time I can remember. It isn't contextualized or qualified. It is presented simply as a stark fact undermining absolutely any instinct, desire, sense of self, dream, feeling, perception, ambition, or inner truth. If you feel something at all . . . red flag. No to intuition. No to what your body knows. No to what your gut is telling you. No to what you want. No to any hunger. No to what feels right. No to what feels wrong.

No to your deceitful, incurable heart.

What source of authority are we left with when the enemy of goodness and truth beats inside our own chests? When we cannot trust our own instincts, whose do we trust instead?

Church people are urged to trust only God, and according to the lying-heart narrative, he wants whatever the opposite of our desires suggests. Since God's feelings about any given thing are a real damn mystery, the shortcut is to go inward, feel around for any impulse, then assume he wants the opposite. If it feels right, it is wrong. If it feels wrong, it is probably godly. If you experience intense cognitive dissonance, let your mind suffer. There isn't a reliable molecule in our horrid human bodies.

Several other verses are cherry-picked with regularity to back up Jeremiah:

> *Whoever wants to be my disciple must deny themselves.*
> *To die is gain.*
> *I no longer live.*
> *Do not love the world or anything in the world.*
> *Those who belong to Christ Jesus have crucified the flesh with its*
> *passions and desires.*

An older, wiser reading can find metaphor and hyperbole, historical references and allusion in these ancient words, but they are not taught this way. As I form my worldview, this truth emerges as immovable:

> *I cannot trust a single thing I think or want.*

I wear a Christian T-shirt to high school, one of many I own. Inside a giant red flame are the screen-printed words "On fire for God." So faithfully will I let my every desire burn, I will become nothing but ashes.

Best Friend

July 13, 2020. I haven't slept in two days. I walk out to my porch somewhere around 4:00 a.m. The world is quiet and dark and somehow still spinning on its axis. How? How dare it? How could it?

I sit on my porch stairs and close my eyes. I feel tender toward myself all of a sudden, like a mother. This is unfamiliar, as I've functionally been my own meanest critic as long as memory serves. I am disapproving, never satisfied, never generous. I push and demand; in the Me vs. Me war, no one has ever won.

But a feeling begins washing over me, full of light and the gentlest, dearest love. It finds a distant memory in my body, an echolocation of nurture I trace in my mind:

I am in sixth grade, a month or two past the Mrs. Anderson disaster, the picture of awkwardness. I am still rattled. I am like a newborn baby giraffe—all limbs, no grace. I clomp around physically and socially. I just can't figure any of it out.

Two of my friends, Amy and Julie, invite me to the county fair. *At night.* This is the sort of thrilling social scenario the movies told us to expect. Unsupervised boy preteens will be legion. I obsess over what to wear, what to say. I comb my short feathered hair until I resemble something between a middle-aged accountant and a softball coach. We are getting dropped off, for shit's sake. We are practically adults.

The fair has all the trappings of an after-school special: overstimulating lights, cotton candy machine, rigged games, the greasy sweet smell of funnel cakes. We aren't there ten minutes when two of *the cutest* boys a grade ahead of us start circling. We see them, they see us, we see them seeing us, they see us seeing them see us. It is a whole thing. We are obviously about to fall in love and kiss next to the Tilt-A-Whirl. The movies were right.

I check myself in the funhouse mirror, adjusting my red dangly earrings from Claire's since Mom relented on pierced ears after the Mrs. Anderson mess (sad moms get real permissive). I clean my glasses and straighten my banging sweater vest. I. Am. Ready. The boys walk over and the flirting begins, which is to say I stand there mute as a statue while my friends giggle and flip their hair. We are thrilled. This is going fantastic.

As we await our cinematic moment, which I assume will happen on the Ferris wheel, the boys grab my two friends by the arms and run off to the left. Not sure if I spaced out and missed the plan, I fumble behind them trying to keep up with the county-fair adventure. Where were we going? What is happening?

I'm not sure but I stay on their heels until I hear one of the boys say: "Why are you here with such a dork?? What an ugly four-eyes!"

They laugh and speed up, looking at me over their shoulders and ducking behind the tents.

I realize they are running away from me.

I gradually slow down and lose them in the crowd. I stand there alone for what feels like an hour. They are gone. I am shocked and devastated and embarrassed beyond comprehension. This *is* an after-school special but I am not the love interest; I am the ugly left-out nerd. My body is both on fire and ice-cold. I am all alone. No one here knows me or loves me. I have no idea what to do.

With every ounce of constraint, I try to hold it together and dam the torrent. I walk around the fair by myself, looking at nothing. My throat is so, so tight. Withheld tears burn as I blink and blink and blink them back. I finally walk to the entrance and sit on a bench. It is eight fifteen. We are getting picked up at ten. All I want is my mom. I wait by myself until 9:58 when my friends walk up, flushed with giddiness and talking over each other.

"Oh my god, Jennifer, like, where did you go?"

But they rush on recounting every arm touch and cute response and carnival ride with the boys before I can answer. They fill the car with nonstop laughter and the visceral thrill of sixth-grade male attention. I stare out the window and beg myself not to fall apart. I count the streetlights we pass, trying to hold in sobs. As Amy's mom pulls onto my street, I bite my bottom lip until it bleeds. Tears are wavering on my lashes (and I'm out of suppression). I yank open the car door before we are at a full stop, and I run to my house.

My mom, mercifully, is sitting on the couch. I stumble to her and collapse on her lap. I don't know how she understands a word I am saying, but I gasp the story out in between heaving sobs: the boys, the names they called me, how they all ran away, how I was alone the whole night. Dad walks in to find me and Mom weeping, my head in her lap while we both unravel, me from humiliation and Mom from the brutal heartbreak of parenting. She strokes my hair and wipes her tears and mine, and—the statute of limitations has run out, so I can disclose this—swears to run those boys over with her station wagon.

I remember thinking: "I just want to stay in this house where I am safe and loved." The cold, lonely feeling of the fair receded with my head in my mom's lap on our tan corduroy sectional with my dad hurriedly making us Coke floats in our familiar kitchen, because emergency dessert is his comfort specialty.

I am home.

I belong.

I am protected and cherished and known here.

This. This is the remembered feeling in my chest and bones and stomach as I sit on my porch at 4:00 a.m. This impression of safety, that *home feeling* after being somewhere lonely and cruel. I have a sense of deep care, that I belong, that I am protected and cherished and known here. But it isn't with my parents at my childhood home.

It is with myself.

This is instantly the most true thing I have ever known.

I physically run my hands gently up and down my arms. I hold my face between my fingers. I wrap my arms around myself and say out loud: "I am my own best friend. I am safe with me. I am home."

I go inside and sleep for fourteen hours.

Addendum: Mom

The *very next day* after the county fair, Mom brought me to the optometrist to get contact lenses, because sad moms get real permissive.

Hidden Corners

It has been three days. I am in a fog of shock and pain and confusion. Nothing, absolutely nothing, makes sense. Despite my mom's best efforts, I haven't eaten. My sisters have slept in bed with me, one on either side, a sibling fortress still no match for the night terrors.

I am in the process of investigation and discovery, and it is physically traumatizing. Here is my actual life on the page, on the screen, in the files, in the accounts. There it is. Not what I thought it was or wanted it to be or even pretended it was, but what it is. Every hour is worse than the last. My skin feels peeled off; I am exposed and raw. I need an emergency room. I need a time machine. I need a miracle.

Three days ago as my husband was leaving with a bag, I said, "The next thing I will hear is either the whole truth or goodbye. No other words." So it has been silent. To be fair, those are two weighty options. We have lived somewhere between the whole truth and goodbye for four years and called it a marriage—only half honest, only half here—so neither of us is anxious to finally make (or hear) a choice.

The whole truth is a real mindfuck for most of us, because it doesn't have any hidden corners, and I personally love hidden corners. They are perfect places to tuck hard things away from scrutiny, away from requiring any attention at all. Hidden corners offered me a mechanism to lie to my own self, because I didn't want the whole truth. *I didn't want it*. I wanted what I wanted, what I'd hoped, what I'd crafted.

I wanted the story of our marriage, not our actual marriage.

Hidden corners harbor unwanted truths; they are very reliable in that way. Use them judiciously and you can fool everyone including yourself. Just take the pieces that hurt and harm, the embarrassing and shameful parts, the ones that humiliate, the bits that indict ourselves, our partners, our relationships, and our favorite systems, and shove them out of sight entirely. The corners are a hermitage for the truths we fear most:

I have an addiction. I am having an affair. I am lying. I am experiencing abuse. We've stopped having sex. My child is in trouble. I am not actually straight. I have a secret life. Our marriage is broken. I don't believe this thing anymore. I've done something terrible. I want something different. I suspect something scary. I am in real trouble with money. My partner is violent. I am drinking too much. I am deeply unhappy.

You can see the need for hidden corners. Facing the whole truth creates a clear before and after, and most of us fear the after. The before may be debilitating, but at least it is familiar. The corners allow us to continue the charade, which is not as nefarious as it sounds. Most of us don't hide the truth because we are unrepentant liars. We simply know the truth will disrupt it all—the life we've built, the marriage we have, the image we've nurtured, the career we enjoy, the approval we've secured. Admitting the truth, hearing the truth, confronting the truth is all highly consequential.

We want the story of our lives, not necessarily our actual lives.

And to be sure, the whole truth will end the story and begin something else entirely, something real. Now, culture supposedly puts a premium on "being real" until it doesn't, which we know. Being real isn't actually cute; it's no aw-shucks with a shoulder shrug. It goes well beyond its saccharine forward-facing version of being *such a hot mess* and *you guys know how I am* and *raising teenagers, am I right?* That type of real is rewarded, because it doesn't actually threaten the story. That is easy real.

Hard real is the whole truth, and that will disrupt a life as we know it.

•   •   •

I receive a text on day three: I am ready to talk. About everything.

Turns out I'm not. The whole truth is looming too large once it is finally an option. It is coming to me already in pieces and I'm not ready to hear it from the voice I've trusted for twenty-six years. My body goes ice-cold, and I shake so hard I drop my phone.

I need one more day.

The following day, we meet in my outside office in the backyard. The two-hour conversation is mostly the whole truth. I listen with my legs drawn up and a pillow clutched to my chest, a useless force field against the trauma. Who she is, her age, her job, where he met her, every detail more shocking than the last. The money spent, the devastating time span, the substances, the lies. Taking her to our lake house, on our boat, the hunting lease, out on public dates. The gifts he bought her, expensive and endless. The cash liquidated without a paper trail, which has no bottom.

"Please tell me everything. I can't keep finding out more."

"Jen, I have lied to you every day for two years. I can't even remember what was not true."

Somehow despite these decaying ruins, there is one part forever worth remembering. Ten minutes before our agreed upon time, I get a text from my two best friends' husbands, Tray and Trace, as dear to me as brothers:

We will be parked outside your house the whole time. We'll just sit in the car. You have to do this part by yourself, but we are thirty feet away. We're here. You're not alone.

Sometimes the whole truth gets scaffolded by the remaining love elsewhere. We may have to bear it, by choice or by force, but the whole truth only shatters the fraudulent parts, not the beautiful ones. Sure, a truth and a lie can no longer coexist once exposed—terrible news for the hidden corners—but truth is no threat at all to whatever else is true, whatever is noble, whatever is right, whatever is pure, whatever is lovely, whatever is admirable—anything excellent or praiseworthy— these are truth's bedfellows, and turns out, they can hold an entire life together.

Mr. Berman

All the eighth graders agree that Mr. Berman is, collectively, our favorite teacher. He teaches science, but aside from that black mark, he jokes with us like we are peers. We love it. He takes us seriously and doesn't talk to us like we are clueless middle schoolers. He lets us get away with cursing, and once he skipped the lesson altogether to talk about the Def Leppard concert Keith Goodall and Katie Franklin went to because they had cool parents. His favorite stance is to lean back in his chair with his arms behind his head and cross his legs up on his desk. He is casual and relaxed, unlike our PE teacher, Mrs. Roberts, who, we also all agree, is the worst.

We like Mr. Berman because he gets us.

Not only does he talk to us about our lives, but he asks about boyfriends and who is dating who and how our parents respond. Sometimes he keeps us, the girls mainly, after class or writes us a pass to miss some dumb assembly or whatever. He invites us to hang out in his room during lunch; we pull chairs right up to his desk. I find myself talking about the boys I like. Mr. Berman is always interested.

Special attention from a favorite teacher is a particular drug for me. I have been historically obsessed with pleasing my teachers, but just through good grades and good behavior. I've always been good at being good. But Mr. Berman thinks I am intriguing, which is unfamiliar flattery. And well timed, because I am a new student this year, back to

Kansas, stunned at the sophistication of my peers. A bunch of them are having sex already. We are thirteen! They are light-years ahead of me. I am a naive diaper baby. I don't understand what they are talking about half the time, but I laugh like I do. Mr. Berman's attention suggests I am pulling off the ruse. He finds me mature and obviously capable of serious conversations with a grown-up.

Around midway through the year, Mr. Berman leans over my desk to point something out, and I experience an unfamiliar prickle at my hairline. I don't know what it is, this feeling. It spikes without my consent. It keeps happening, like my body is separate from my mind. I am not deliberately thinking any thought, but I see him make long eye contact with a girl, and my chest feels hollow. He sends me out the door with a tight hug, super normal of course, obviously, and the backs of my hands tingle, which always happens when I'm nervous. He cracks an adult joke, and I have the strangest urge to cry. He suggests hanging out during lunch, and something feels bad in my stomach, which is ridiculous because it is just Mr. Berman. He loves us.

I don't know how to process my body's involuntary response to his proximity. I don't understand it. I guess I am being paranoid? Or hormonal—I did finally start my period this year, and you know what everyone says about emotional girls and their periods. My unease happens over and over, though, which is so unfair to Mr. Berman. Since there is nothing wrong with him, something must be wrong with me. There is no other way to interpret the data. I am giving myself faulty intel. My body has gone rogue.

I am visiting home my freshman year of college. My best friend Amanda comes over and we go for a long walk. We are college girls now. *We have seen things.* Let us tell our tales away from little sisters and eavesdropping parents. The wide-open air will give us plausible deniability. We venture into sexual territory; it becomes a confessional walk. I am spinning my yarns when Amanda goes quiet. I've probably said too much. We were stars of our high school youth group and I've sullied our legacy. I prepare to retract some details when she says:

"I am actually in counseling about some sex stuff."

This is 1992. We don't go to counseling. No one goes to counseling. Who goes to counseling? Therapy is only for very, very, very serious problems. I put my hand on her arm. I'm scared about whatever this is. "Do you remember how I started babysitting for Mr. Berman?" she asks. I do. Amanda got the coveted invitation into his real life, his real house. "He . . . did stuff. Mainly when he drove me home. He kissed me and . . . touched me. We were so close, and it was confusing and I didn't know what to do. I told my college professor and she got me into counseling. I'm kind of fucked up from it."

I learned two things that day:

1. That was what predatory grooming looked like.
2. My body always knew.

Falls Creek

It is 1997, and we are baby adults in our first grown-up jobs. The ink from my diploma isn't even dry, and I am in charge of 30 fourth graders and my husband is in charge of an entire church youth group. Well, *we* are, really. His job is my second job. In student ministry, the wife is part of the package deal, but that's neither here nor there.

Summer youth camp is our Super Bowl. Southern Baptist Oklahoman teenagers only go to one place for church camp: Falls Creek. It is historic, iconic. Hundreds of thousands of kids have passed through its portals into ministry, the mission field, the marriage bed. It is the bedrock of regional evangelical adolescence. Every youth pastor we know (legion from our university training ground) will drive his students there in poorly air-conditioned buses to post up in the same rustic, church-owned cabins their parents went to. Each week of summer camp will host five thousand kids and their pastors, interns, volunteers, and Kitchen Moms.

The apex of each day is evening chapel in the monstrous outdoor tabernacle. It is heartfelt and impassioned, the location of endless salvations, rededications, surrenders to ministry, and full-on emotional meltdowns. Additionally, it is where students decide who to hook up with from other youth groups. In other words, the epitome of church camp.

We are walking our crew to the tabernacle, everyone freshly

showered and buzzing from a day of shenanigans and canoeing and emoting. As we approach the building, I see one older man and woman stationed at each entry point. About to pass through with our students, the woman puts her hand on my shoulder and stops me:

"Your shorts are an inappropriate length. You need to go change."

The kids all freeze. I look down at my Old Navy khaki shorts maybe three inches above my knees, mortified.

"What? These??" And in some desperate attempt to salvage my dignity, I add, "I am the youth pastor's wife."

"Those"—she points at my shorts, unmoved—"are *in*appropriate." As if I've forced her to further indict me against her will, she holds her hand sideways at my knee to show that, see? These violate the four-finger gap.

I glance sideways and see girl after girl being flagged and sent back to her cabin. Every one of them, truly, the picture of modesty. Prepared to encounter God, we are instead singled out and shamed, as if our motive was to seduce every male away from his rightful spiritual experience with our slightly-above-the-knee flesh (or shoulders). We are brazen. We are thirsty. We have no discernment or decency. The boys walk in with impunity.

I come back in a maxi skirt. I can't remember what the sermon was about.

Journal

I put pen to page long before understanding this is how I make sense of the world. It starts young with short story masterpieces stapled together with construction-paper covers (colored-pencil illustrations also by the author). I write plays and notes and rhyming-only poems and, in one notable instance, "It is always best to tell the truth" five hundred times for swindling my sister Lindsay out of her allowance to buy a stuffed unicorn at the gas station.

Like all daughters of the '80s, I also keep a diary stashed under my mattress complete with lock and key. I store my quietest feelings there, the ones that lack an outside voice. I try out some curse words in the safety of hidden pages. I disclose my obsession with a series of boys well above my station; I don't have the looks but definitely have the eye, the worst asymmetry. I practice several new last names to see which one looks the dreamiest in my bubble cursive.

This is also the place I journal penance to God, who features very prominently in my psyche. I don't think of him as *loving* so much as *watching*. An astute student, I've assimilated the job description of his favorite prototype. Good behavior has come naturally to me, so I feel committed to hitting my marks.

Unfortunately, I keep getting sidelined by forbidden desires. I fixate on boys and love and kissing. I'm supposed to cherish "my citizenship in heaven" and of course "do not love the world or the things in the world," but I keep accidentally loving so many things in the world. I am smitten with the delicious possibilities of a big, juicy life, and I can't seem to help it. With thoughts like these, I am in real danger of God's disapproval or maybe even damnation, and I ask Jesus into my heart about once a week to cover my tracks.

The deep inner truth is that I want road trips and fresh summer peaches and sandy beaches and beautiful stories. I am positively breathless at the idea of love and longing and sex; being desired is seismic. I have some unnamed big hunger inside me—dreams or power or ambition or something—and I fantasize endlessly about becoming the sort of person who is worthy of it all. I want to live. I want to chase these desires straight into a gorgeous life. This is all so real in my bones.

I don't know how to tell God I love the world.

So my journal entries sound like this:

God, I am so sorry for not putting you first. Help me get rid of everything but you.

God, please forgive me for thinking about boys. I only want your love!

God, help me serve you better and stop thinking of myself. Help me stop being so selfish! This life is not about me!

God, I'm so sorry for disappointing you again. Help me try harder!

God, I want to bring you joy! Show me how to make you happy!

I am a child begging for mercy from an abusive parent who can't be pleased. I contort my normal desires around a tyrannical gatekeeper in charge of my eternity. My prevailing hope is to become less, because my largeness threatens the enterprise. After all, God called us to holiness, not happiness. I know the system.

. . .

Fifteen or twenty years later, I mention all this to a friend who grew up Episcopalian:

"I had to love only God and hate the world."

"Oh, that's so weird. Because the Bible says God absolutely loves the world. I wonder why you were taught you had to hate what God said he loved?"

Porn

We sent our five kids to church camp every summer, because of course we did. We went as teenagers, we took our own youth groups in the '90s and '00s, and we insisted on camp for the youth program when we started our own quirky little church. Youth camp is just part of the deal. Plus, our spawn had the "enviable" title (sarcasm font) of "the Pastor's Kids," so their spot on the bus was SAVED.

Having never forgotten my too-short-shorts citation of 1997, we ensured the camp we chose had no history of misogyny or overt patriarchy. We scoured camp websites looking for signs of egalitarianism, reading the fine print to make sure they weren't secretly affiliated with fundies. We would absolutely not stand for men telling our girls how to dress, act, and speak, and if there weren't some women in leadership, our little youth group would take their zealous little hearts elsewhere. They could sing "Oceans" somewhere woke. The girls would not be targeted if we had a say. Men and boys had been spiritually centered since, well, Earth's beginning, and whatever camp we chose would not pile on to that narrative.

So imagine my surprise when my *son* finally admitted his camp experience years later.

"Mom? Want to know where I learned about porn? Youth camp in seventh grade. And not the way you think, like from other dudes. Every night, the camp leaders took the middle school boys out to the fire pit and said, 'Who here watches porn?? If you won't admit that you do, go back to the cabin.' I went back every night, Mom, because I had no idea what porn even was! I didn't know what that word meant. And every night, they kept saying those of us leaving were lying. On the fourth night, I finally just stayed because I was so embarrassed. I had no idea what they were talking about, but I could tell I was doing *something* wrong. Then they spent an hour telling us how dirty and filthy it was, and that God knew what we were up to. And how we were ruining our future marriages. So the minute I got my phone back, I googled 'what is porn' and *then I found out*."

My insides got very still and quiet. I remembered the plucked rose, the dead stick, the accusation that we were dirty, filthy girls ruining our future marriages. I looked at my son's face, this good-hearted boy shamed for sexual curiosity he had barely even exhibited. I imagined him feeling wildly embarrassed but not sure why, hyperaware of his body and burning with shame. I envisioned him nervously glancing at the other boys, wondering if they knew they were all such a problem. I pictured his cheeks flushed with humiliation.

At age twelve, they were already accused of spoiling their wedding night. Apparently, there was no coming back from being a depraved, dirty porn watcher. Good luck finding a woman who wants to marry a pervert.

At the onset of adolescent sexuality, he heard:

Boys' curiosity is gross and needs heavy policing.

Boys are hopelessly deviant.

Boys should be scared of God.

Boys are responsible for a pure bedroom.

I was so busy looking out for the girls, I forgot to look out for the boys.

Why weren't we vigilant to protect our sons too? Purity culture doesn't just cripple girls sexually; it is equally devastating for boys. The through line is *shame*: same song, two different verses. When the overarching message is that sex, sexual curiosity, sexual experimentation, sexual thoughts, and even sexual desires are inherently wrong, no one can be right. There are zero winners in a system that pathologizes normal, natural sexuality. None. It doesn't leave the boys unscathed. They are no more curious than girls are, but purity culture assigns deviance to their emerging sexuality and forbids it entirely for the girls. Either way, they are all forced into hiding, now afraid of their own desires, their own bodies, their belonging, the adults, and God. Sex is vilified before they've even thought about experiencing it.

I know it because I lived it too.

A ship taking on this much water ought to be abandoned and left to sink.

Judy

Because I can't sleep, eat, process, or function, I am working with Judy, who is, well, she is an energetic body healer. Very woo-woo. My girlfriend Laura, who specializes in alternative healing practices, booked and paid for this session, because my friends will do anything to help bear this pain. I am lying clothed on her table, acupuncture needles placed just so, her hands moving strategically over my belly, my hands, a particular amount of time spent on my head.

I have used my brain to alchemize everything I've ever experienced—I am an internal processor—but currently my mind is only a poisonous loop of trauma. I am trapped inside thoughts and images like a prisoner with a life sentence. So because I cannot rely on my cerebral partner, I am forced to listen to my body. Perhaps she will be a more gentle guide. Maybe she knows something I cannot think my way to.

Judy is walking me through a visualization while her hands explore the energy in my body:

JUDY: Where are you?

ME: I am at the bottom of the ocean. I am drowning.

JUDY: Can you kick to the surface? Get your head above water?

ME: Okay.

JUDY: Do you just want to tread water awhile? Would that
          adrenaline still serve you?

ME: No. I don't want that.

JUDY: What do you see? A raft? A life preserver? Can you reach for it?

ME: I don't want to be in the water at all anymore. I want to be on the shore.

JUDY: Can you see it? Can you swim to it?

As she works her hands over my head and body, I try for three or four minutes to get to that shore in my mind with tears pouring down my face while Judy keeps gently wiping them away.

ME: I can't get there. It is too far and I am too tired.

JUDY: Okay. What else do you see then?

ME: Oh. A boat.

JUDY: Who is in it?

ME: Everyone who loves me. All of them. They came for me.

JUDY: Can they get you to shore?

ME: Oh my god. Yes.

And in my vision, my people haul me into that boat and row to shore with all their collective might. They place me on that blessed dry land, that warm sand, and wrap me and the kids in blankets and surround us with safety and love.

I made it. I didn't die as expected. Shockingly, I lived.

And right there on that table, I wonder if I have permission to stay on the shore—a feat of hubris since I am drowning every minute of every day. I am sunk, with no evidence that safety is remotely close or ever coming. The data does not suggest I am going to survive being lost at sea. My brain repeats the doomed analysis ad nauseam.

But my body seems to know something my mind cannot grasp yet. It is like she is saying gently: "Follow me." What if I can choose the shore? What if I am able to stay on solid ground with my beloveds in safety? What if I have the capacity to bury my feet in that warm sand, wrap that blanket around my tired shoulders, feel the safety of solid ground under me . . . and live?

I decide to trust my body for the first time in my living life.

Jeep

Spring 2014: Our oldest son, Gavin, has secured the first driver's license in the Hatmaker squad, a day I expected to dread until I realized he could pick up milk and ice and little brothers from soccer. A third driver? In a family of seven? Licenses for all! Give one to the fifth grader!

This kid is all ranch, all boy, all Hays County. Gavin is deer blinds, dirty boots, and meetups at the water tower. He is a country music song. We drive a used Jeep onto our property in the middle of his sixteenth birthday party, hand him the keys, and don't see him for two months. He and his buddies, the same since fourth grade, take the doors off and burn up every mile in the hill country.

One night he comes in rattled with that look teenagers get when they are on the ropes, dodgy body language that suggests parents should prepare to hear a tale. The story will immediately be too long and contain thirty-one unnecessary details. My husband and I are standing in the kitchen when the fiction begins:

"So what happened was that Joseph and I were driving back in his neighborhood—well, we were *both* driving because we were going to pick up Trevor because his mom needed the car because hers is in the shop to get, like, a new suspension I think? So we were maybe going to leave Joseph's truck for him to use but I'm not sure about that, so he drove just in case. And you know Joseph's neighborhood is all back

49

roads and there are, like, *no* streetlights, because I guess they voted against them because of light pollution or something, but we were just driving normal. So Joseph was in front of me and, um, I think, like, a deer ran out, and also he hit a pothole, so I swerved, because *I* didn't want to hit the pothole too, and because it was *so* dark because of the no lights, I guess I ran over a fence and tore up someone's property a little with my Jeep."

(Teen translation, reader: They were mudding in a field and ran over a fence.)

Gavin is never in trouble. He's the classic oldest child. At this moment, his face is stark white, *translucent* white, and he is so visibly nervous, I think he might pass out. Boys doing donuts in a country field is the exact brand of trouble I want from my teenagers, but we are the adults and the parenting contract says we are supposed to make a deal out of this. So we start in tandem giving stern rebukes about safety and speed limits and the appropriate use of a free car. In no uncertain terms, we let him know the "deer" and "pothole" are bullshit and he is an atrocious liar. He and Joseph will fix that fence, yada yada yada. We are tag-teaming like pros.

The problem is that neither of us is really mad, so we are running out of steam fast. Our tough act is losing its luster and we can't think of anything else to say, particularly since Gavin is on the verge of a meltdown. His obvious distress is hilarious to us, because we are bad people. We catch each other's eyes and know immediately in that married-for-twenty-one-years way that we are about to crack and someone needs to be the hero, so my husband raises his voice one last time and bellows:

"Gavin, do you know what a car is for??"

Gavin is mute, frozen, pale. He can't even answer.

"TRANSPORTATION!"

That's it. I can't take it another second. I drop to the floor behind the counter and try to muffle absolute guffaws. I am at laughter-in-church level. There is no recovery. I am no longer a participating parent in the phony discipline scheme. I have to crawl out of the kitchen back to our bedroom on my hands and knees. My husband drops his voice and laugh-whispers to my retreating back: "How dare you." He sends Gavin to his room with the remaining four seconds left in the tank before bursting. We howl until tears roll down our faces.

It is the smallest memory, a blip in the whole life we built, but I love it.

No one will ever know those five kids like we do.

No one else shared the moments.

We are the keepers of the family stories.

We know all the shorthand.

We were a team.

I've lost my institutional memory partner, and that loss cannot be quantified. No one else will ever remember the fake pothole. They weren't there.

Memory

I don't want to see you or feel you,
I don't want to look into your eyes.
I don't want to touch you or miss you,
I just want to love your memory tonight.

-Miranda Lambert, "Love Your Memory"

"For Grief"

I am finding shock a paralyzing force.

My husband chose someone else, a *shocking* someone else.

Nothing can compete with this information. It overrides my system in every stratum. I can't stick with any other train of thought long enough to matter. The number of times I've declared through the years that infidelity would *never* happen to us is infinity. It just wasn't possible. We loved each other too much. We were too protected. We'd done the right things. We followed the script.

The way this new knowledge feels in my bones is so painful, I can't believe it hasn't killed me. I've now seen pictures and texts that feel unsurvivable. They play on a relentless loop across the screen of my mind, terrorizing me. I'm trapped.

My friend Rob sends a text:

> Here is a link to a meditation app called Simple Habit. Use it. It will help you get back into your body. My favorite narrator is Cory Muscara.

I will do anything to escape my mind prison. Hell, I will try Orangetheory like a sociopath if someone tells me to. I download the app and forget about it for a couple of days. My mind is a sieve; anything helpful slides right through, leaving only the sludge of misery. I can't hang on to anything good.

My house has been a hive of activity every second of every day, for which I am profoundly grateful. No quiet rooms to envelope me, no lack of bodies or words or motion. Nonstop chatter and tasks. No silence for my mind to start the story over yet again. I want it this way. I want it like this for a minute.

But a few days in, all of a sudden I know: I need to be by myself, if only for an hour. I feel it. I am my own best friend, and I need me. I crave the peculiar safety of the privacy of my soul. Where the only sorrow to manage is mine, and I don't have to temper a thing.

I decide to just drive. My car is a private moving room. I have no place to go but I'll just go somewhere, anywhere, nowhere. As I slip into the driver's seat, not sure how to access the enormity of my pain, I have the innocent thought to play a guided meditation as my driving companion, a focus aid for my emotions. I scroll through the app and choose one simply titled "For Grief"—no need to get complicated here. It is only eleven minutes. Okay. This will get me started on my country drive.

I hear the first gently spoken bit as I back out of my driveway:

"When we lose someone we love, it's natural to feel grief. Grief in a way is exactly the correct response to loss. It's a beautiful natural feeling. The idea in grief meditation is to allow the feelings to be there. Just allow them to naturally arise in your body right now, and begin to feel the body sensations of grief as they arise. You may feel a kind of pain in your chest region. You may feel a lump in your throat. You may feel various sensations of wanting to cry or brow furrowing or lips curling in your face. You may feel many other body sensations. Whatever emotional sensations you are feeling in your body, just allow those to be there. Feel them deeply. Encounter them with clarity, openness, and allowing. Let's just do that right now for a little while."

My brain was only going to listen, but my body instantly accepts the permission slip. I drive exactly eleven houses up the street, and I am unable to go on. I pull under my neighbor's huge pecan tree, put my car in park, and start screaming. I weep and sob and wail from the depths of my wrecked heart. I am inconsolable and out of my mind. It won't end. If a neighbor sees, they will call an ambulance. I lose all time. I have never physically grieved like this before or since.

I sit under that tree in my car screaming for almost an hour.

I allow everything. I don't tamp it down or speed it up. I don't ask it to have more dignity. I don't let myself feel afraid of this violent sorrow. I experience the suffering in my chest and back and head and stomach. Agony cascades from every place my body has stored this trauma. I let it run down my face and soak my shirt. I let my fists beat the steering wheel. I let my howls pierce the air. I rub my wounded heart with my hands and hold myself like a best friend. I wail like it is the only thing that might save me.

I bypass my mind and give my body the gift of grief.

Ironically, it is my first moment of relief.

Lindsay

We are somewhere in our twenties, me upper, my sister middle. I've done the thing: young marriage, three kids by twenty-seven. Lindsay spent several years deeply in love with a pilot who never wanted to get married, didn't believe in it. He'd stay in a relationship with her for infinity but rings would not be involved. An outdated institution, the failure rate, a long list of objections. Until he broke up with her and got engaged to someone else within the year. I am in the morning-mayhem routine with preschoolers and toddlers when she knocks on my door at 7:15 a.m. bearing the engagement news, brokenhearted, sobbing. I cancel my day.

Why is it so hard to tell the truth about marriage?

It is a few years later, and Lindsay has fallen in love with a different man. We don't know him. He lives in a different state and they met through this person and that person and a few degrees of separation. She spends an unusual amount of time giving us his personality résumé, like she is making his case. We will surely love who she loves, so this feels unnecessary, but yes yes yes, we believe you. Not your type but good, we believe you. Hard to read but kind, we believe you. She burns miles up and down I-35 building something outside our purview.

She is engaged. There is a ring and a venue and plans. I've seen the dress and the veil but haven't yet met her person. In our family, when one of us has a person, the rest of us know that person. But to be fair, there is complicated geography. And I am raising three little humans and this is all explainable. We buy bridesmaids dresses. Lindsay picks out a menu. She chooses a cake. Operation Wedding Planning rolls on.

In that shorthand sisters have, I start to read her silences. Where an exuberant response belongs, there is a glance away. In place of enthusiasm, tight smiles. She dodges my questions. Her answers get small. She gets small. Something is wrong.

There is that thing in families where our early roles dictate our adult dynamics, even if they are no longer accurate or true to our lives. My textbook role thus far has been Oldest Child; Lindsay, Second Oldest. I ran the typical tight operation assigned to firstborns, and Lindsay did whatever the opposite was in every category. I had goals. She had fun. I was voted Most Inspirational. She was voted Biggest Flirt. I was a prude. She was a party.

Thus my married, three-kid, mortgage-having worries would be seen as bossy, or worse, disapproving. How dare I question her discernment and threaten the security of her story? I cannot be the sibling who throws doubt on the biggest decision of her life. Our other sister maybe. Our brother perhaps. But not me. My job is simply to be thrilled for her. But I am genuinely scared, and I am positive she is too. Something is wrong. Neither of us can admit this to one another. We don't want to disappoint each other.

Why is it so hard to tell the truth about marriage?

Five weeks from the wedding, the invitations go out. They are on the refrigerators of our aunts and uncles, our neighbors, our best friends, all the bonus parents who raised us. Final arrangements are made. Hotels are booked. The rehearsal dinner is planned. Deposits are paid. This wedding is imminent.

My dad, braver and truer and far more loving than I have been, calls Lindsay with four weeks to go and says: "Honey, we could be at the back of the church about to walk down the aisle, and with one word, we would call this off. Mom and I can take care of everything."

For the record, Dad could have prioritized a dozen other things: money, appearances, all the trappings of being a big fish in our little pond. It was a lot to unravel; hundreds of calls to undo a wedding on next month's calendar. But Dad had also watched Lindsay getting small, and no nonrefundable payment on earth was worth losing her.

But the real hero was Lindsay, who heard confirmation of her own instincts, who later told us she would be a verbally abused wife in Oklahoma had she married him. Rather than continue to tell a lie about an impending marriage, she told the truth, past the approved expiration date. The wedding was canceled. She chose herself. It was the right and good and brave choice, and everyone else's expectations could just burn. No one else would be living her life. No one else would experience that marriage. No one else would have slowly lost themselves inside a lie.

But Lindsay saw exactly what her future would have been. *She knew.* There was what it looked like, then there was what it was. Despite being the lead character in a season where every element of your relationship is glorified, she held the truth with tighter hands and refused to abandon herself to a story, however lovely it appeared. Instead of doing what was expected, she did what was right. She saved herself.

It is indeed hard to tell the truth about marriage.

But some people do it.

Remy

Of my five kids, four of them primarily operate inside the social rules I modeled. They learned to smile politely regardless of the merit of the conversation, or the conversationalist. They nod and affirm and respond with graciousness. To spare a millisecond of someone else's discomfort, I taught them to swallow their dissension until later; we let that loose away from watching eyes. We hold our tongues in polite company. Our manners are legendary. We understand how the social engine needs to be greased, and we are ready with our oil.

We are so fucking pleasant.

Then there is my youngest.

Remy is built differently. She was born with a pure heart in a confusing, unscrupulous world. None of its sharp edges make any sense to her. She cannot speak sarcasm, irony, or rancor. If your body language is not aligned with your words, Remy is baffled; passive aggressiveness will never land. When you say one thing but mean another, she will take you at your word, not your implication. She is completely, fully, and only: earnest.

So when she doesn't understand something, which is often, she asks directly, no matter how intrusive or embarrassing or ill-timed. If she can't read your plain meaning, she will not, under any circumstances, act as if she can. While the rest of us can read the room, read between the lines, read a face, and then follow the social script accordingly, Remy has never even understood the scene.

This, historically, has proved quite a conundrum for me.

Her lack of social skills is in direct conflict with my obsession with being well-behaved. Her responses suggest I didn't teach her to prioritize the comfort of others. I become short-tempered and exasperated. I cut her off and talk over her questions. I overexplain her reactions to provide escape from the awkwardness.

Sydney said to me recently: "Mom, sometimes you are triggered by Remy." God, I didn't know anyone could see that. I thought I was masking my discomfort, but apparently I only reserve that skill set for strangers. My therapist said triggers are clues revealing something important, something that needs attention, something not yet neutralized since it is still easily detonated. The trigger isn't about another person; it is about me.

I've given Remy so many scripts, thousands. None of them stick. They are social fillers forgotten the minute she texts them, or speaks them, or writes them as dictated.

But what if Remy has it right and I have it wrong?

What if the appropriate response to this duplicitous world *is* confusion? What if bewilderment at social choreography is the only true thing happening in the room? What if decorum doesn't grease the machine but grinds it to a halt? I've never lived in a world where we all say what we actually mean and feel and think and believe and want. Maybe she is the one standing in integrity and the rest of us are just following the damn script.

Lighthouse

No one knows what to do for me, but they don't want me to be alone.
So I'm not. Not for one second. For four solid weeks without missing
a day, my mom is on my porch with her coffee by 8:00 a.m. waiting for
me to walk outside into the stifling summer air.

"Mom, you don't have to be here this early."

"Honey, I can't bear you waking up in this house alone."

My dad hasn't slept in a month. My sisters are cleaning out closets
and drawers and boxing up size 11 shoes. My brother is mowing my yard
and scrubbing my grill and grieving the first brother he ever had. My
best friends are in a campaign to make sure I have a text, call, visit, or
snack once every eight minutes. They are all hovering over me, and I
am hovering over the kids. None of us can staunch the tears.

Divorce breaks a million hearts.

Jenny and Tray call me over for a night on their porch with our
friends. We are tap-dancing to make any thirty-minute stretch feel normal. Between these four couples plus me, we've been married a collective 126 years, no divorces. Our grown kids took baths together when
they were in preschool. We have lived a Chosen Family life together for
over two decades. Our squad has never experienced a breach. We have
no muscle memory for this. I am determined not to suck the oxygen
out of the room; I practice telling a joke like a fun friend. I can be regular for two hours. We are all exhausted.

Someone is telling a story, a delicious moment of normalcy, a tiny break from the grief deluge. Everyone laughs. I'm so grateful to be out of the spotlight. Sinking into the shadows, I chuckle and nod along and then realize tears are streaming down my cheeks. My eyes are involuntarily crying despite my brain's express lack of permission.

Bodies won't be tricked out of mourning. They know too much.

I focus on staying silent so the tears might pass unnoticed. My friend Andrew spots me across the porch, his military training attuned to changes in the atmosphere. I shake my head almost imperceptibly. He pauses, considering my nonverbal request, then makes an on-the-spot decision not to leave me alone in my pain. He looks up at the clear summer night sky, the suffocating air weighing heavy on all of us, and then locks eyes with me and says this:

"Jen, when I was in the navy, we *lived* for the day we would finally get to shore. It was all we wanted after being at sea for so long. We would stand on the deck and watch for land, squinting as hard as we could, and at first, from so far out, all we could see was one tiny light, usually a lighthouse. But it was just enough to know we were getting closer. Then a few more scattered lights would come into view. Then we'd start seeing the barest outline of a few buildings. We'd finally make out windows and people and signs of life. And before long, the whole city was in view and we were home."

The porch has gone silent. We are all desperate for a single hopeful word.

"You can probably just see one tiny light right now, if at all, and it is so far away. But keep watching. Please keep going. You'll see more lights and more land and signs of life soon. The shapes will come into focus. It will become clear and beautiful again. We all know it.

"You'll get home."

Hearts

If I bring you home to mama
I guess I'd better warn ya
She feels every heartache I go through

And if my dad sees me crying
He'll pour some whiskey over ice and
Tell a lie and say he never really liked you

Oh, if we break up, I'll be fine
But you'll be breaking more hearts than mine

-Ingrid Andress, "More Hearts Than Mine"

Super Bowl

I am in tenth grade at church on a Sunday morning per usual. We miss church never. How Mom gets four kids there every weekend in the requisite dresses, tasteful flats, and pink-sponge-rolled hair is a mystery. The drive there in the station wagon is always perilous. Someone is painting clear fingernail polish on a run in her pantyhose. Someone is eating Cracklin' Oat Bran out of Tupperware because they didn't get to breakfast in time. At least two kids are fighting about seat placement and body adjacency. Someone is whining to go back because they forgot their missions offering. We have sometimes more than but no less than three meltdowns every Sunday before walking in the double doors smiling.

After Sunday school, we all go to Big Church. For unclear and unwise reasons, the youth group sits together front and center, directly in front of Brother John while he preaches. This unfortunate proximity is made that much worse by the watchful eyes of the entire choir behind him. The choir loft features a one-hour popcorn effect of various parents in blue robes giving the death stare / scary finger point at their kids passing notes on the church bulletins and laughing during the service. My mom, Nicki's mom *and* dad, Jill's mom, Scott's mom: We get silently threatened by all of them. It takes the whole choir to keep the youth group from misbehaving.

Near the end of the service, after the alter call but before the offering, Brother John issues a charge:

"As you know, tonight is the Super Bowl. While I'm sure some of you will choose to watch it, the faithful folks will be here tonight for the five o'clock service. What's one game compared to eternity? You think God will ask you who won the 1990 Super Bowl someday? I'll be here and I'm praying you make the same decision."

I've mastered this calculus. The more you give up = the better Christian you are. The amount of fun you forfeit is proportional to your faithfulness. There are two well-rehearsed evangelical lists: what to do, and what not to do, the second outpacing the first by a multiple of a hundred. The list of behaviors required to please God is clear, and church attendance is certainly included. People notice. Tallies are kept. Godliness is ranked. Heaven is certainly watching.

I know "the joy of the Lord is our strength," but sometimes it seems like joy is more located in a rowdy football party with chips and cheeseburgers and funny commercials. It is like the whole world gets to have fun except us.

I guess we follow God until every enjoyable thing we ever wanted evaporates.

Holiness, not happiness.

I skip the Super Bowl for Sunday night church.

Front Porch

April 2020. We are one month into a global pandemic, which we barely have language for. What we do have is a bunch of kids at home trying to figure out the earliest days of Zoom classes on the two laptops among us. We have puzzles. We have short-lived optimism toward invented structures like Family Outdoor Movement Hour, block schedule for homeschool, organizational projects (roll eyes here). My friend Trina institutes "Family Master Class," where each person is responsible for presenting some interesting content to the rest of them. This lasts one and a half weeks.

Our home life is already brimming with tension. Red flags abound. The kids and I are exclusively at home. My husband is, confusingly, gone a lot. Gone when the entire world is going nowhere. Gone well past the family errands he volunteers for. When I ask why Find My Friends is disabled on his phone, the one he never, ever sets down anymore, he is perplexed: "Maybe something about our coverage?" He comes to bed after 2:00 a.m. most nights. Liquor is appearing and disappearing on our bar every single day. Everything, absolutely every-thing, feels wrong.

Alerted by a racket one morning, I find him crowbarring up our whole front porch. We live in a 1908 pier-and-beam house, so he is standing three feet below our front door threshold where the porch used to be. In an hour, the entire structure is demolished, rendering our front door useless.

"It's fine," he assures me. "I'm going to rebuild it this weekend."

Three months later, he is gone. The porch is still a gaping hole. We haven't been able to use the front door since that day in April. I stare at the razed project, smashed in a blaze of dysfunction, left unfinished, untouched, unfixed.

It is a full story.

At first, I'm unable to make plans, make progress, or make money. Hell, I spend the first few weeks just trying to get anything to make sense. No porch or workable front door is the least of my problems. But eventually it bears noticing: "We, literally, have a broken home."

My husband has been gone for almost two months. As the whole truth sinks in, it becomes clear that I can't fix him, and he can't fix me, and on a blistering call, he adds our marriage to the list of unfixable things.

But I am determined to fix *something*.

My best girlfriends are not counselors or psychologists but something better: handywomen. Like, handier than all the men I know put together and doubled. Jenny and Shonna have a design business and taught themselves everything: carpentry, electrical work, plumbing, demo, tile work, sewing, furniture making. Nothing intimidates them. They can unbox an IKEA dresser in seventy-three thousand tiny unknowable pieces and put it together in twenty minutes.

"Can you help me rebuild the porch? I need this."

The speed at which they attack this project is staggering. In under an hour, we have a carpenter, lumber order at Home Depot, and stain picked out. My front yard becomes a workshop of buzz saws, electric drills, and sanders. The handywomen are measuring and taping and cutting and, well, I don't really know because I specialize in typing for a living. Plank by plank, the porch is reemerging.

On the last day, in 105-degree temps, my sons and mom and sister join us, and we ruin eight outfits staining the new porch on our hands and knees, the smell of freshly cut wood permeating the yard. Ben sands and refinishes all four rocking chairs. We paint the new trim and rails. The girls style the whole porch with a new rug, bright pillows, fresh lamps, and—purely temporary since I've never kept a plant alive— two lush hanging plants with tiny periwinkle flowers.

It is pristine.

We stand in the grass—filthy, sweaty, covered in sawdust and stain—and realize the porch is 100 percent more beautiful than before it was demolished. Through tears, I stare at the completed project, constructed in sheer love, now finished, embraced, fixed.

It is a full story.

Telluride

It is September 2020. The world is in chaos. My kids are the COVID School Generation, a club they neither wanted nor thrived in. Two of them lost their senior year endings and graduation ceremonies in May, one is forfeiting her university film project, and one gets to start high school and the other his junior year on borrowed Chromebooks at home.

Additionally, their dad moved out July 11.

We are altogether sunk. When I look at photos from this time, every one of us looks exhausted. We wear our sorrow like a wool overcoat in summer. The kids are all with me; I am the home parent, the full-time parent, which I remain permanently. There will not be a reconciliation effort. Our marriage is over. He tells me clearly that "trying requires certain feelings to be there" and they aren't anymore and they won't be coming back and that is that. The connective tissue of love and like is gone, and rebuilding on sand is a fool's errand.

To save a marriage you have to want to.

It took another year to admit this, but when I put the question to him and his answer was "Call your lawyer," I was . . . relieved. I put up not one word of appeal. I hung up, cried for an hour, then didn't shed another tear for a week. This is such a strange paradox to explain, because he caused such trauma and there will never be an excuse for it. No amount of disconnection warranted an ending like that. The punishment categorically did not fit the crime. I didn't deserve it. None of us did. So conceding that our marriage was over felt like absolution for a while, and I wasn't willing to grant it.

It was strange to process the loss of my entire known life. On one hand, I couldn't eat or sleep. I was *racked* with grief. My days began and ended with mourning. On the other hand, turns out I wanted our marriage to be over, same as him, just not like that. I did not want him to say "Let's work on it." We'd been the most distant of bedfellows for almost four years. Anything beautiful about us had evaporated from the searing heat of death, trauma, career loss, and booze.

We didn't lose our marriage that July, the night I woke up to those words. We started losing it years earlier but couldn't face it. A combination of losses converged: Our careers in Christian leadership ended abruptly, he endured a series of complicated surgeries, and our friend died in a traumatic accident. Rather than bring us together, this concentrated season of pain drove a wedge that sent us to our respective corners; he became unrecognizable, even to himself, a slow atrophy of hope, integrity, and will. I offered a bright face on our behalf, but no one was fooled except me when I wanted to be.

In some ways, I knew this was happening before It Happened. We all did. Family members and friends had already broken the implied agreement of denial and asked me through tears: What is wrong with him. Where has he gone. What is going on. What do we do.

In other ways, I didn't have the faintest notion. *Not the faintest.* It was ten million times worse than I thought. It was beyond thoughts I have ever even thought. It was a full Category 5 hurricane that had already wiped out the entire coastline while I made sandwiches and pretended it was a sunny day. By the time I turned my face toward the horizon, there wasn't a single house left standing. I didn't believe the storm warnings. Those usually amount to nothing.

And here instead of listing the uninteresting story of middle-aged male disintegration, I instead examine my role in the necrosis of our marriage. I had become so profoundly resentful, so exhausted from the daily land mines of his unresolved trauma, I just . . . left. I mean, I was there, doing the things and managing the things, but even if he would have reached for me—did he reach for me?—I was gone.

I became his roommate. We stopped having sex, we stopped connecting, there was barely a scrap of tenderness to be found. It must have been lonely for him too. Gone were the basic efforts to see and hear my partner. I just wanted him to get his shit together but didn't offer to walk the long road home with him. Didn't offer to carry his bags for a while. Didn't demonstrate compassion when his grief came out as fury and his fear as constant criticism. I relocated all relational intimacy to my friends, family, and kids. I threw myself into rebuilding my career while his was in rubble. I lived a full life largely adjacent to him, and after a while, I forgot our marriage was ever anything more. The time to grab hands had passed. After all, to save a marriage you have to want to.

He called it: time of death.

With that, the manic agony gave way to a quiet, low-register heartache. I looked at the kids and grieved their loss down to my bones. Losing the stability of your parents' marriage in high school and college is annihilating. Any dream they ever had about coming home to us, bringing their friends and partners and babies, was dead. Sure, they could visit two houses, but who dreams of that? Right as childhood neared its end, the one thing they counted on, their safe place to land, their forever home, collapsed.

My friend Laura sends a text: My girlfriend Kelly has a beautiful vacation home in Telluride, Colorado, and she wants you and the kids to go there. You can stay as long as you'd like. This is a gift. Take it.

"School" is starting in four days, virtual only. Remy is a freshman, Ben a junior, Caleb delayed from the military, Sydney a junior at the University of Texas through a computer screen, Gavin managing a two-thousand-acre ranch in Alabama with his new college degree he didn't get to walk across a stage for. My assistant has already canceled my foreseeable calendar under the descriptive label "Crisis." Everything is triaged. We have to physically be nowhere. On the spot, I decide we are going for two weeks. Somehow we leave within twenty-four hours.

We abandon the relentless heat of a Texas summer with suitcases full of sweatshirts and Chromebooks and I don't even know what else because planning is well outside our capacity: "Just fill a suitcase and we'll see what we have when we get there." Sydney and I mostly bring books. Ben and Remy bring their virtual school tools, which I later find out were put to zero use. We get to Telluride by the skin of our teeth.

I could natter endlessly about what Colorado means to me, what it has meant to me my entire life. I grew up very middle class, so "vacations" were simply not a part of our repertoire. My first airplane ride was on my honeymoon. But my family had two aces up our sleeve:

1. My Grandma and Grandpa King bought an A-frame cabin near Colorado Springs with a view of Pikes Peak when I was in elementary school.
2. My dad was a minister of recreation, which included organizing a church ski trip to Crested Butte every year, and our family got to go for free.

Functionally, this meant we drove our unreliable VW van across I-70 from Kansas to the Colorado Rockies every summer to the cabin and every winter to the slopes (back seats removed so we could lay our sleeping bags on the floor because '80s). It is the only place I ever traveled my entire childhood. And if you think I feel cheated out of geographical diversity, think again, Jack. The smell of pine trees, the eyeball patterns on the aspens, the crunch of the gravel road leading to the cabin, taking the Silver Queen ski lift up to Paradise Bowl, then over to Ruby Chief first thing in the morning on a snowy Colorado day . . . utter, utter enchantment. What a childhood.

Colorado is the scene of ten thousand happy memories. It raised and nurtured me since I can remember. It means family and road trips and card games and wool socks. It is playing horseshoes with my grandpa and his best friend Hoppy, who built a cabin across the street. It is greasy cheeseburgers at the Paradise Warming House at the base of Crested Butte fresh off a morning of skiing, hands frozen, slope tales being told and certainly exaggerated. It is long johns and freshly showered hair and hot chocolate in front of the fireplace at night, faces windburned, boots dripping melted snow all over the front hallway, counting the hours until the ski lifts open again in the morning. Colorado is happiness and beauty and my favorite place on earth.

Annie Dillard wrote in *Pilgrim at Tinker Creek*: "Mountains are giant, restful, absorbent. You can heave your spirit into a mountain and the mountain will keep it, folded, and not throw it back as some creeks will. The creeks are the world with all its stimulus and beauty; I live there. But the mountains are home."

The kids and I limp all the way to Colorado, and we heave our spirits into the mountains. We rent bikes and read books; we ride the gondola and eat brick-oven pizza. The kids each make dinner one night, including homemade "Crunchwrap Supremes" by the boys, which take two hours and cost ten times that of their inspo order from Taco Bell. We watch the entire sucktastic season of *Cobra Kai* piled in my bed while

Caleb declares: "Sweep the leg of alcoholism, Johnny!" Ben and Remy pretend to do virtual school and I pretend to care.

We cry, which is honest and true. We laugh, which feels like a bona fide miracle. I keep touching their skin, staring at their faces when they aren't looking. I listen to them laugh and talk trash while we play Spades. I study their body language and watch them walk side by side in front of me. I pay attention like it is my gainful job. I see them being them. There they are. Here we are. We are ourselves. Here is our little family acting like we do. We have each other and we are still here. We are okay. We are going to be okay.

At the end of two weeks, I stand in the middle of the street, my face toward the majestic box canyon of Telluride, tears running down my cheeks, and whisper: "Thank you."

I decide to wake up and live.

part two

THE
MIDDLE

Steve

I have no idea how much money I make. I don't know what or how much our bills are. I don't know how many credit cards we have or their balances. I am hazy on our bank accounts with no clue on the passwords. I do not know how to file taxes, quarterly or otherwise. Don't know our lenders. Have never seen the numbers on our lake house. No idea on savings, retirement, investments, or beneficiaries. The most rudimentary financial investigation reveals a disaster of unspeakable proportions.

I am a foolish walking cliché.

I text my friend Lindsey, a wealth planner, and ask for advice. On what? I don't even know. I guess every single thing that exists financially for a grown-up. She sends me to her boss, Steve.

I drive downtown to his beautiful house-converted-to-office on West Sixth Street with my laptop in hand. I'm sure I should have brought statements or bills or whatever paper trail depicts the state of the union, but I don't have any. I don't even know what to say or ask or do. So instead I sit at his cozy round table, open the water he hands me, and burst out crying. An impressive start.

He asks the most basic questions. I can answer none of them. Genuinely, none. I am shocked and ashamed at my ignorance. What the hell have I been doing all this time? How could a forty-six-year-old with a big career be this irresponsible? This is humiliating, especially for someone who teaches independence and autonomy to women. The numbers tell a very true, very alarming story about my life, and I never even bothered to look.

After the twelfth unanswered question, Steve passes me a tissue and quietly shuts his laptop. He is so kind, so dear, so gentle sitting across from a woman unraveling in real time. He gives me my first square feet of solid ground:

"First of all, you are going to be okay. Do you hear me? You are not doomed. You can and will learn all of this. You are smart and capable. This is knowable. This is doable. I am going to help you. This is a new start, and heads up: You can trust *yourself*."

This is about money and also not about money. He is one part financial planner, one part big brother, one part therapist, one part pastor. I want to slow slide onto the ground with gratitude. Steve hands me my first message of security, and it cuts through the fog of fear. I don't know what I expected coming in here, but those few sentences alone are worth it. It is not too late. It is not too hard. I am not too stupid. This is not too impossible.

"I am giving you a list. Work on these alone. Then come back in ninety days and we'll get down to business."

- Go through every bill: home, cars, utilities, credit cards, boat, tuition, service providers, insurance, subscriptions, everything. Write each one down, including the provider, balance, payment, due date, interest rate, and account information.
- Put every bill you are responsible for in your name.
- Open a new bank account. Set up auto bill drafts. Change your auto deposits.
- Close every shared credit card, and take a new one out in your name.

- Refinance your home in your name.
- Meet with your CPA on your tax history and next steps.
- Cancel all frivolous subscriptions.
- Clean up your spending. No unnecessary purchases for three months.

I am physically dizzy. I take deep cleansing breaths just to absorb this task list. I am at the rock bottom of a mountain so tall, I can't see the top through the clouds. I actually don't know how to find some of this information. Plus, I have a historic aversion to what I call "up fronts": receiving the whole scope of something at the beginning of a longer execution schedule. As a student, I'd famously melt down every time I read a syllabus at the start of a semester. I am flattened by "goal meetings" spanning the next calendar year. Instructions with multiple complex steps send me to the fainting couch.

This financial literacy task list might as well be written in Hebrew. Sitting in my car in Steve's parking lot, I allow myself a dramatic cry. I sob tears of embarrassment, shame, fury, humiliation, fear, overwhelm, and loss. Financial management is not an uncommon division of labor in a marriage, but I have absolutely been sleepwalking. I am stunned at my irresponsibility. Not only was my lack of partnership around money unfair to my husband, but it allowed for an unaccountable disaster. I can't even find the bottom of his illicit spending.

I drive home with my list, sit at the dining room table with my laptop, light a candle, take a huge breath, and call my bank: "Justin, this is Jen Hatmaker. Can you help me?"

Amy

I was always scared to be home alone when my husband traveled. Irrationally so. I'd lie in bed on high alert for every sound, every creak, every obvious sign that someone was breaking in. Nights when he was gone, my bed companions have ranged from bats to knives to a cast-iron skillet because it seemed, with the right swing, it could really fuck someone up.

In my close-friend stable, I have two very woo-woo girlfriends and it is a toss-up which is more granola, Laura or Amy. In this corner, we have breath work, sound healing, star charts, and Ayurveda. And in that corner, an alternative buffet of crystals, herb therapy, Chinese medicine, and energy healers. They regularly say things like "He is giving very low vibration" and "Well, Mercury is in retrograde, so . . . "

They have invited me on energetic wellness retreats, called in an herbal order when the flu swept our house, sent quizzes so I could get my doshas identified and balanced. I love it. I love them. I love their chakras and yoga and plant-based medicine. I love how they double-check what day and exact time I was born to ascertain my issues. Never underestimate having a couple of witchy friends.

· · ·

Amy sends a text:

> I am coming to smudge your house. I learned in my Reiki course. I need you
> and the kids to be gone at least four hours.

Laura already sent me to Judy the body healer, so my two celestial
friends are delivering exactly as expected. I have obviously never had
my home smudged. This house was renovated on HGTV, for Pete's
sake. It was a commercial enterprise to entertain the masses. We didn't
have smudge sticks; we had cameras. But I'd also never done acupuncture and energetic vision casting, which unlocked my body for the first
time in existence. So smudging? Sure. I make up some reason for us all
to be gone half the day, and we clear out.

It is disorienting when your safe space becomes the scene of trauma.
Which is it? The shelter from the storm? Or the storm? This right here
is where I was when I found out. This was where I ran. This was where
I screamed. This was where he sat all those late nights outside my view
texting, calling, drinking, lying. This was where his clothes were, our
picture hung, his office was. This was where we lived when he left us.

"Will you move?" everyone asks.

"I don't know," because I don't know.

Amy is Jesus woo-woo, a churchy witch if you will. She hangs red
curtains the whole month of December, and once when I was over with
Christmas music playing, she got quiet and said: "Coming to us as a
poor baby. I just can't believe that is how he did it."

Amy spends several days preparing to smudge my home, including
gathering specific prayers for every room. She knows us all so well, and
she also enlists my mom and other friends. Caleb's prayer is different
from the kitchen's is different from mine. The living room couch needs
its own plea. Negative energy has soaked every baseboard and window.
The house is drenched in strife.

She sends me her notes afterward:

I felt like a conduit the whole day. The corner of the couch was so sad and scary and I kept getting sent back to it. I was exhausted after, like I had been completely used up and wrung out, but in a good way. I slept forever when I got home but felt completely at peace and protected during that recovery.

I started out by opening a window in each room. I sat in the living room and did a five-minute meditation. I lit the candle, prayed for guidance, turned on Gregorian chants, then began.

I visualized all the tension, fear, sadness, anger, bitterness, and despair that was created—things I could feel when I walked in—that had settled into the corners and still spaces. I played a chime in each corner of every room.

"Dear Lord, please release any negative energy trapped in the corners of this space. Clear out the darkness to make room for Your love and light and loving-kindness."

I lit the sage bundle and started by the front door. For each area, I used a prayer. I walked around every wall using my turkey feather to spread the smoke.

> *"Dear Lord,*
>
> *With this sacred smoke, bring about:*
> *Light and the start of the new day*
> *Warmth and strength for growth*
> *The closing of this day and season*
> *Wisdom and guidance for the future."*

I went upstairs and repeated the whole process. Then back downstairs, I lit a piece of palo santo wood. Going in the same order, I sat in the middle of the floor and prayed over each room.

Amy sends the exact prayer she blessed each room with, including these:

Dining room [which, amazingly, my brother Drew built by hand]: *Holy Spirit, embody this smoke, fill this space, and bless the gatherings that happen at this table. Be present for every person, in every communion. Let the lumber of this table ground this home into the foundations of the earth and the steadfastness of Your love. Let the love that Drew poured into these boards be an anchor that holds the people that surround it.*

Master bedroom: Holy Spirit, embody this smoke, fill this space, and bless this place of rest. Let Jen feel respite, renewal, peace and comfort here. When she lays down her head, quiet her mind. Let her rest. Let her sleep be complete and restorative. Let her dreams be cathartic but not traumatic. Please, please let her sleep.

Upstairs (Jen, your mom gave me words to pray over the kids' rooms): Holy Spirit, embody this smoke, fill this space, and bless this place of solitude. Fill this room with loving-kindness, peace, joy, restoration and abiding love. Let them feel their grandparents' love, Your love, Your control, and Your sweet comfort.

Living room couch: I went back here again. I took the throw blanket outside and gave it a good shake and left it in the sunshine awhile. Sat on the coffee table and faced the couch. Holy Spirit, embody this smoke, fill this space, and bless this place of heartbreak. Take away the deception, shame, lust and despair. Do not let this furniture hold that darkness. Redeem this small spot that has harbored such pain. Fold this small spot back into the heart of this home, and reclaim it for the whole family.

The house smells like sage for days. Amy reached into the divine energy of the universe and restored our home.

•　　•　　•

Two things become clear, one immediately and one over time:

1. I am not moving. This home feels clean and pure and safe again.
2. Since that day, I have not gone to bed scared one single night. Not once. I never felt nighttime fear again.

Porch Swing

I am developing a new relationship with my old house. At first, it was "ours" and "before," but somehow it is becoming "mine" and "now." I bought his half. The kids and I are figuring out how to live snugly in this new configuration. I'm painting cabinets spring green and peacock, and in a blaze of hubris, a fuchsia master bathroom with oversized floral wallpaper. I'm changing out pictures and pillows, barware and rugs. I create a cozy library nook the readers fight over.

One night, I come home after being out of town, and my oldest son says, "Mom, leave your bag right there and follow me."

"Why? Where?"

He leads me by the hand out to our covered side porch that spans the whole length of the house, the scene of so many gatherings it is considered "an additional living space" on our survey. I look to my left where the couch, oversized chairs, and mounted TV are arranged, the section where we congregate. It is quiet and dark.

Gavin slowly spins me to my right where all my best friends are surrounding a gorgeous porch bed swing hung with braided ropes and stacked with cushy pillows and blankets. I have been asking for exactly this for a decade.

"*Oh my word.*" I cover my face with my shirt and begin sobbing. I run to the swing and lob my entire body. My girlfriends built it from scratch and signed their names on the back with this message:

"Hope you have years of good wine, good coffee, and good friends, and you feel Jesus near to you every time you sit here. -Jenny, Shonna, Megan, Trina, Sarah, Laura, Christi, Julie"

Hysterical, I wrap my girlfriends in my arms and admit to already being in love again.

With them.

Car Blind

The thing is, I married a car guy. We then spawned car sons. Additionally, I am car blind. Every car is the same car to me. Sedans, hatchbacks, small SUVs, crossover cars . . . identical, every last one. Furthermore, unless it is fluorescent pink or green striped, every car color is the same color. A white Toyota Avalon is the exact same car as a blue Subaru Outback. I don't know why I have to explain this.

I host a backyard party as a freshly single adult determined not to forfeit all fun. The next day, I notice a white (gray?) car parked in my driveway by my detached garage. The following day, there. Third day, still there. What. In. The. World? I can't *believe* one of my neighbors parked in my driveway that long without asking or moving their car. What if I needed to get in or out of my garage?? Finally on the fourth day, I write a note and stick it under the wiper:

"If you don't move your car by tomorrow, I will have it towed."

That evening I am at Megan and Jordan's—literal best friends—for Friday Pizza Night and I tell the story of the car and my mean note. Jordan reaches into his pocket dramatically and whips out a paper: "Do you mean this note?! On *our* car??"

Reader, I ask you: How am I supposed to know what my friends drive?? I can't know everything. If you wanted me to remember your car, you should've painted it fuchsia. I didn't mean to threaten my friends with impoundment. I'm sorry for what I said when I was car blind.

My point is this: I have never bought a car. Never done the loan, the haggling, the dealership thing. Frankly, I've barely even picked one out. When you live with car men, you just come home to a different car on a random Tuesday. Can all the children fit in it? Does the air conditioner work? Then it's fine. Just give me the keys. I like this black color. ("It's pewter, Jen.") Okay then.

But now, abruptly, I am in charge of my whole life. By myself. I've transformed my bedroom into a feminine, moody oasis involving a melodramatic green velvet bench. I've refinished my original 1908 hardwood floors to their natural gorgeous grain. I am keeping the two front porch hanging plants alive like some sort of damn gardener. I painted several walls black. I turned the front room (previously his masculine, leather-ish home office) into my light, bright "inside" office with a purple swivel chair and promptly rebranded my outside office as a "studio." Everything is my choice. What I keep, what I purge, what I cook, what I decorate . . . and, I guess, what I drive.

My car is fancy and posh. I didn't choose it. I have given it zero minutes of thought. All of a sudden one day, I cannot keep driving it. I need this car to be gone; it is radioactive sitting in my driveway. It feels urgent that I exercise independence here. I've figured out my mortgage, insurance, 401(k), investments, bills, taxes, credit score—hell, I've drafted a will. It is time to be a grown-up and buy my own car for the first time at age forty-six.

Problem: I have no idea what kind of car I like.

Car Son Gavin asks leading questions: *What style do you like? What era? Do you love a model or make? Do you want another SUV or a smaller car? Do you want a new car or used? Is there a color you want? Have you always liked someone else's car?* I blink at him dumbly, like the seagulls in *Finding Nemo*: "Mine?"

I begin car exploration through a highly specialized tool—Google. As in typing "what kind of cars exist" and hitting "Images." I start with a fairly large funnel called Every Car That Was Ever Built. What my approach lacks in strategy, it makes up for in volume. Do I like the Toyota Highlander? How about the Honda CR-V? Nissan Pathfinder? The problem as outlined above is that all of these are the same car to me. I forget what each one is the second I look away.

However, I start noticing what I am noticing, because car noticing is a new skill set. I notice I don't like any of the current cars. They are all "fine" and I'm bored out of my mind with this Google probe. The thought of driving one of these gray/white/black/blue SUVs/hatchbacks/crossovers/sedans (any combination is the same vehicle) is a snoozefest. Maybe I should just get remarried so someone can start buying my cars again.

Until.

My investigation starts revealing a preference. I notice I like beefy, boxy cars. I have a strong aversion to fancy. I don't like the mom cars. I could give a shit about name brands. I like the ones that have a vibe beyond Bluetooth and adaptive cruise. I want a ride with some pluck. I'm less interested in elegant and more interested in moxie. I need something for rolling the windows down and blaring '90s country. I want a manifestation of a woman who lost a twenty-six-year marriage and plans to rebuild a kickass life.

I buy a matte-black 1975 Bronco.

This old girl has an AM/FM radio, hand-cranked windows, and a stick shift. It is giving high school vibes. It is serving vintage looks. It is a *Seventeen* magazine cover with John Stamos. It is top down, ball cap, Ray-Bans, and Shania Twain. Not one thing is automatic, intuitive, modernized, or shiny. It is as loud as a freight train and stiff as a block of concrete.

We were born a year apart, two sisters who've seen a lot of life, taken quite a few dings, have some old parts giving us a bit of trouble. We aren't the newer model, that's for sure. Both of us need just the right touch to get started, but if you learn to speak our language, we'll purr to life for you. At forty-five and forty-six, we've slowed down a little; top speed is around fifty-five miles per hour, but we still manage to get there. We both come stocked with memories and operate old school in nearly every way. One doesn't have power steering and one won't give up her paper calendar. We each belonged to someone else, but now we're on our own; newer versions are abundant elsewhere. The shine is off the penny, but if you like spunk, we're your girls.

I found her myself.

I love her.

We both still have a lot of gas in the tank.

And I never confuse her in a parking lot.

The Prerogative to
Have a Little Fun

Let's go, girls.

-Shania Twain, "Man! I Feel Like a Woman!"

Jenna

My dad is an exceptional teacher and storyteller. He taught a Young Married Sunday school class my entire life. In church lingo, Adult Ones are young marrieds, Adult Twos have kids in the nursery, Adult Threes are wrangling teenagers, Adult Fours are in their grandparent era, et cetera. Saturday nights found Dad studying his lesson with copious notes in his microscopic handwriting, which, fun fact, tipped us off to the Santa scam; "Santa" should have typed his return letters.

Dad is hilarious and irreverent, and he is quite literally everyone's favorite. He created a conundrum for Immanuel Baptist Church in the '80s and '90s because the Adult 1 couples refused to graduate to the Adult 2 class. No one would ever leave. So his class was enormous and included the brand-new baby marrieds, the over-forty-five softball league couples, and everyone in between. He bottlenecked the Sunday school flowchart, not that he ever followed any rules.

Southern Baptist theology dictates that only men lead. In fact, the denomination expels churches with women in senior positions. There are no female preachers, teachers of adults, lead staff, deacons, board members, elders. Women staff the nursery, the volunteer positions, the kitchen, and the support roles. I had no idea women could wield spiritual authority or be gifted teachers until adulthood. I never saw any who did.

. . .

I am visiting my parent's home in my late twenties. I have endless babies and a husband who works seventy-hour weeks, so I drive eight hours alone up the hellscape of I-35 to Wichita for two summer weeks. Between my parents and sibs, I won't give a child a bottle, a bath, or a book once. These are the only grandbabies and they will be reliably overattended.

I tuck my littles into the church nursery on Sunday—so strange to be a grown-up back at my home church—and head downstairs for Dad's Sunday school class. It is overly crowded per usual, and I grab a seat in the back with a few of my favorite rowdy wives.

"Did your dad tell you he got in trouble?"

Look, my dad grew up at this church. My grandpa was a founding deacon. Dad was best friends with Tim Siler, who, fortunately or unfortunately, was Pastor Forrest's son, and the two of them were utter ne'er-do-wells. Once in middle school, they crawled on top of the roof and cherry bombed the church ladies in the courtyard. One of the deacons saw their ladder, took it down, and left them stranded on the roof as punishment (it was a different time). I am just saying my dad has been in trouble at this church since elementary school.

"What did he do? Curse during his lesson?"

"He had Jenna Searl substitute teach for him. Some man called an emergency meeting with the pastor about a woman teaching the biggest adult Sunday school class on campus."

I don't know how to place this information. I'm familiar with limitations on women in church leadership, of course, but I've never seen it challenged here. I am quickly sorting this data into mental categories: Dad, women, teaching, rules. I feel a buzz inside. This has something to do with me but I can't tell what.

After church, I ask my dad: "You got in trouble for having Jenna teach? What did you say to the pastor?"

"I said I didn't give a good hot damn what anyone thought. Jenna is the best Bible teacher I've ever heard. Anyone who doesn't like her teaching my class can kiss my ass."

My dad, Southern Baptist to his bone marrow, the best man I know, defied the limits our theology placed on women, restraints I thought were set in concrete. He gave his seat to Jenna and defended her right and ability to sit at the table. I am shocked. I am moved. A key quietly turns a lock on an internal door and it cracks open.

Two years later I write my first book as a spiritual leader.

Damn Melody (and Brené)

I'll tell you my preference: I'd like to lay this whole implosion at the feet of my partner and walk away clean. It's such a tidy option, and you have no idea how much I love an open-and-shut case. It would make it all quite simple and require no self-examination, super easy to defend, like tapping the right answer on the board with a wooden pointer: "Members of the jury, the explanation is obvious."

But twenty-six years of complex data is giving me some trouble.

Oh, not at first, of course. At first it was black and white, cut and dried, plain and simple; if you follow my pointer, you'll see the straightforward list on the board. And while that first block of time was dystopian, I did enjoy the baked-in absolution. I had a free pass, almost entirely agreed upon and offered to me internally and externally.

The first offender in my recovery process is Brené Brown. Not only does she have the gall to tell me to exercise every day, sleep nine hours a night, and stop drinking so my body won't shut down (I do not listen and my body does indeed shut down), but she tells me to immediately purchase *Codependent No More* by Melody Beattie and consider it my Bible.

Now listen, I'm not a lawyer, but I don't believe we are legally allowed to disobey Brené Brown. I think there is some sort of legislation that requires us to do whatever she commands. So even though Brené tells me she once *threw that book across the room*, I still plunk down $12.75 and purchase my own copy.

Before the book arrives, this already feels like a misdiagnosis. I mean, I don't know what *codependent* exactly means, but it sounds needy, meek, and reliant. It sounds like someone who can't function until her man comes home and tells her what to think and do. It does not sound like someone who has a thriving career and a clear mind of her own. Shit, I keep a thousand planets spinning a day. I mean, I'm not trying to brag, but I have been on *The Today Show* a bunch. Stop asking me about it, you guys!

Guessing I've accidentally given Brené the impression that I am a fragile flower, I open *Codependent No More* to correct her miscalculation. Before I am barely out of the intro, I read this:

> A codependent person is one who has let another person's behavior affect him or her, and who is obsessed with controlling that person's behavior. But the heart of the definition and recovery lies not in the other person—no matter how much we believe it does. It lies in ourselves, in the ways we have let other people's behavior affect us and in the ways we try to affect them: the obsessing, the controlling, the obsessive "helping," caretaking, low self-worth bordering on self-hatred, self-repression, abundance of anger and guilt, peculiar dependency on peculiar people, other-centeredness that results in abandonment of self, communication problems, intimacy problems, and an ongoing whirlwind trip through the five-stage grief process.
>
> Codependent behaviors or habits are self-destructive. We frequently react to people who are destroying themselves; we react by learning to destroy ourselves. These habits can lead us into, or keep us in, destructive relationships, relationships that don't work. These behaviors can sabotage relationships that may otherwise have worked. (p. 34, 37)

This is disruptive and I am only on page 37. Then there is a bit about how codependency can keep others from being well or getting well, and we are all sick from it, and I don't care for this. I wasn't under the impression I would have a turn on the witness stand. Nor did I think any of this would carry forward post-divorce. I thought my relational problems ended with my marriage, of which I was an innocent, a *victim* if you will.

> Once they have been affected—once "it" sets in—codependency takes on a life of its own. It is similar to catching pneumonia or picking up a destructive habit. Once you've got it, you've got it. If you want to get rid of it, you have to do something to make it go away. It doesn't matter whose fault it is. Your codependency becomes your problem; solving your problems is your responsibility. (p. 16)

First of all, rude. Second of all, if "it doesn't matter whose fault it is" is true, that is the basis of my whole case. I admitted evidence, and exhibits A through H should make this an open-and-shut case, Your Honor. And what is this "once you've got it, you've got it" business? I am innocent, Judge. I no longer have the marriage so I no longer have the problem, right? Case closed.

So I flip to the chapter called "Codependent Characteristics," assuming it will clear up this little misunderstanding. There are quite a few. I read the first couple of lists—caretaking, low self-worth, obsession—and think: "See? This isn't really me." I prepare to rest my case. And then: Denial.

Codependents tend to:

- Ignore problems or pretend they aren't happening
- Pretend circumstances aren't as bad as they are

- Tell themselves things will be better tomorrow
- Stay busy so they don't have to think about things
- Become workaholics
- Watch problems get worse
- Believe lies
- Lie to themselves (p. 45)

WTF.

I underline every single subpoint and write "ugh" in the margin. This list is a mirror. By the time July 11, 2020, rolled around, the shit I pretended wasn't happening was so severe, so entirely deranged, we were living in a burning house while I casually made beef bourguignon for dinner. The dysfunctions I kept *from my closest people* indicated I was too embarrassed, unhappy, and terrified to tell the truth. So with outside folks, I was totally pretending.

Inside the family, I bent everyone carefully around his wild mood swings, explosive anger, unseen grenades. When one of us stepped on one anyway, I tried to control (his) behavior and (their) responses. It wasn't fine, but I tried to make it fine. Our marriage wasn't fine, but I pretended it was. The kids weren't fine, but I told them they were. He wasn't fine, but I treated him like he was.

I mine my memory for patterns and don't have to look far. I married a person who was not easy. He wasn't bad, just hard. From the time we started dating and every year since, I managed people's difficult experience of him, including the kids. If he was mean to someone, I'd do a cheerful tap dance to lighten the atmosphere, then make excuses, explanations, and amends behind closed doors. I tried to rearrange the molecules so people wouldn't experience what they were actually experiencing. I gave it the old razzle dazzle.

And of course the reprimand I'd then dole out to him: "You hurt her feelings." "You need to apologize." "That was rude." "You're a pastor. You can't snap like that." I don't mean to give away the content, but Melody Beattie would say this is "codependent behavior," which, frankly, I'd be fine with if it worked, but it is resoundingly ineffective. I tried to manage perceptions, soften someone else's blow, and then privately criticize behavior to patch the whole mechanism. To my surprise, no one appreciated (or believed) this voluntary labor and it changed nothing ever, except to deepen resentment between me and my partner. This dynamic was one of our most recurring battles.

Then adding to this outward management, I became increasingly distant, which, upon later examination, was also an attempt at control via punishment. If my verbal censures wouldn't work, perhaps emotional disconnection would: a sign of my clear disapproval. I began embodying the very negativity I resented.

Turns out, I wasn't just an innocent bystander caught in someone else's unresolved issues. Codependency actually makes things worse—not better, not even neutral. I wanted to preserve relationships, reputations, experiences, and goodwill, but codependency overpromises and underdelivers. In an attempt to "save," it is getting too close to someone drowning after they slashed their own life jacket. They are flailing and dangerous, and they will drown you trying to keep their head above water.

Now imagine that person has been self-drowning nearly every day—for months or years or decades—and you attempt the "save" over and over and over and over and over and over and over and over. I ask you: Which of these people is more in need of reform?

The premise of ending codependency is simple: Each person is responsible for him- or herself plus all the consequences.

Yes, even the person drowning.

I struggle with the concept of self-responsibility. Because people actually die and destroy and traumatize and create misery out of their own misery, and this is not small. The mere idea that the drowning person has to quit slashing their life jacket and reach for the ladder feels heartless at best and inconceivable at worst; after all, not only is this person in trouble, but they are causing real harm. If not for their sake, what about the innocent people they are grabbing onto?

Ask any mom who has sent her child to rehab for the sixth time after he pawned her grandmother's jewelry. Ask any spouse of an alcoholic after parenting the kids through yet another violent meltdown. Ask any child of a gambler who blew her savings at the tables. Or drop it lower to gateway codependent behaviors: the parent still making appointments for her twenty-six-year-old; the resentful spouse pulling all her partner's weight at home; the person who gives a friend a third loan after another financial misstep.

What kind of person lets someone drown, even from their own choices? How can we not try to fix what is broken in someone else, especially if they are breaking other people? This idea struggles for footing in my life not just as a woman raised in the patriarchy but as a Christian raised in evangelicalism. "Helping" has been our presumed mission since time immemorial, but we are not helping the self-drowner; we are attempting to control them. This is their work, and our frantic intervention only delays that possibility while keeping us in a perpetual state of anxiety, anger, victimization, and trauma.

Beattie writes:

> Control is an illusion. It doesn't work. We cannot control alcoholism. We cannot control anyone's compulsive behaviors. We cannot (and have no business trying to) control anyone's emotions, mind, or choices. We cannot control the outcome of events. We cannot control life. Some of us can barely control ourselves.
>
> People ultimately do what they want to do. They feel how they want to feel (or how they are feeling); they think what they want to think; they do the things they believe they need to do, and

they will change only when they are ready to change. It doesn't matter if they're wrong and we're right. It doesn't matter if they're hurting themselves. It doesn't matter that we could help them if they'd only listen to, and cooperate with, us. IT DOESN'T MATTER, DOESN'T MATTER, DOESN'T MATTER, DOESN'T MATTER.

And that's the truth. It's too bad. It's sometimes hard to accept, especially if someone you love is hurting him- or herself and you. But that's the way it is. The only person you can now or ever change is yourself. The only person that it is your business to control is yourself.

Detach. Surrender. (p. 79)*

*Melody Beattie, *Codependent No More: How to Stop Controlling Others and Start Caring for Yourself* (Hazelden Publishing, 1986, 1982), 34, 37, 16, 45, 79.

Self-Appointed

I am the first kid, first daughter, first niece, and first granddaughter in the extended King family. Growing up with my sisters and cousins, I am always the teacher, the doctor, the mom, the president, the choreographer, the director, the emcee, the lead singer, the preacher, the librarian, the stylist, the producer. I make up the game, craft the story, and assign the roles.

Turns out I like to control other people.

How else can you get the ending you want?

Hanky

When the history books chronicle the timeline of my generation, there will be about a ten-year period that meant very little to most of the populace but everything to a handful of us: the blogging era. Between the late 2000s and early 2010s, Al Gore's internet handed ordinary writers a place to hone their craft, and while we were doing that, we built a whole community. Between the blogs we wrote on WordPress and the dozens we followed, creating and reading online writing was a full-time gig.

It was during this time I harnessed my internet power to force a few extraordinary women into becoming my friends. I loved their writing from afar first, then I finagled my way into their hearts. They never stood a chance.

Fast-forward ten years, and six of us outlasted our medium: Kristen, Sarah B., Jamie, Tara, and Sarah G., plus me, turned ourselves into a loyal coven. We started in five different countries and are now concentrated between Texas, California, and Canada. I don't have enough words in this book to explain all we've been through, everywhere we've traveled together, all we've held for one another, but for our purposes here, three of us ended young marriages to pastors in the past five years, me being the last (the other three girls have husbands people write love songs about).

I drag my shattered life to their safe arms.

Through the miracle of Voxer, they are my daily sorority. Their messages range from practical—"My lawyer suggested . . . " "Make sure you . . . " "Don't forget to . . . "—to something closer to gang warfare— "If I ever see him . . . " "If he so much as likes a post of mine . . . " "I know a guy." Perfect girlfriend behavior, obviously. As I told all my friends this year: "I need to take the high road, but I expect you to take the lowest road that exists. I don't want to so much as glimpse your faces on the high road."

I get a small parcel in the mail with a Canadian return address: Sarah B., the most spiritually attuned and earnest among us. I peel back the brown paper wrapping and find a paper-thin vintage hanky with tiny hand-painted red and purple flowers. It smells like peppermint. Tucked underneath is a letter from Sarah in her perfect cursive:

Dearest Jen,

Since everything fell apart, I have been anointing this little cloth with oil. Each time I do, I pray for you. I am sending it to you now, soaked in prayers and the Word. I know it might seem weird but consider it an icon of prayer and love, all for you.

Because when all is said and done, the last word is Emmanuel: "God with us." Isaiah 8:10.

At your side always. I'm proud of you. You are who we knew you to be. Jesus is ever more than we could imagine. I imagine you, held in the love and embrace of God, who broods over you like a mother.

P.S. This is one of my own granny's hankies. It works nicely for crying and waving.

If you think a prayer-and-oil-anointed hanky that belonged to Sarah's Canadian granny isn't enough to see you through another day, you've never received one, I can tell you that. Blessings, blessings, blessings, they keep coming. Somehow they keep coming. One at a time, just on time, they keep coming, sunlight making it to the forest floor.

The Boy Template

A trope of the patriarchy is that it harms women while serving men. Yes, it harms women. Yes, it serves men. But that is an incomplete list of its victims.

Being a mom of three sons is illuminating. Ask the global community of mothers about their boys, and a different story emerges. You will hear about sons that love dance and music and beautiful stories. Some boys are gentle as lambs. Others wear their sensitivity like a cloak and respond to the world with unrestrained compassion. There are shy sons, cerebral sons, gay sons, creative sons. Boys are not just one thing any more than girls are.

A fixed power differential is absurd for all of us.

I think compassionately now about the template my ex-husband was handed. We were students at a conservative Baptist college with rigid gender expectations. As a freshman, I knew the stencil and was prepared to master it. I'd been trained. As I arrived, he was starting his junior year having just "changed his life for God" that summer after spending his first two years partying on a basketball scholarship (athletes were exempt from the purity culture as long as they were securing championships).

So during my first week of college, he was also finding his renovated place in the ecosystem not as an athlete with a free pass but as a fresh, new "ministry major" with a prescribed character sketch to learn. The male superstars on our campus were scruffy, good-looking, Doc Martens–wearing alphas who organized Bible studies and guitar worship sessions by the fountain. They didn't drink and led all our campus clubs and ministries. They were charismatic, confident; tons of them were studying for the pulpit. Their North Star was clear.

These boys were revered and could have married any one of us; girls outnumbered boys there seven to one in 1992. We wanted in. Most of us had been groomed in the art form of Being a Pastor's Wife and were prepared to be *darling*. It was a given that the boys had "callings" and their careers would be prioritized.

I met him when he was trying with every fiber in his being to become that guy. He'd only had six weeks of practice when he first spoke to me in the Geiger Center. His effort to be a different man was at an earnest fever pitch, so it read like a perfectly delivered script to me: the right words, the right demeanor, the right authority. Say less, my man. He would lead and I would follow. Our mold was set.

But what happens when the prescription is all wrong for that boy and all wrong for that girl? What if that boy splinters inside hierarchal leadership, and that girl is actually powerful? It creates a big fucking mess, I'll tell you that.

Furthermore, what if even the most assertive, authoritative men are *still* not meant to dominate their spheres? The imbalance of power inside marriages, churches, companies, governments, and systems has a long rap sheet. It is the source of centuries of abuse and misery. Though the men appear to be winning, they are not. Patriarchy robs the whole earth of flourishing.

Not only does it reward a narrow male job description, but it punishes those same men for suffering. When they experience complex trauma, which they do, their pain is perceived as weakness. In America, twice as many women go to therapy as men do. And of the men who go, they take twice as long from the onset to seek treatment. In the years before my marriage ended, as he went through a quick succession of losses telling the world he "was fine" and we believed him even as he slowly disintegrated.

The patriarchy failed him too.

Looking back, I wonder what would have happened if we met even one year later, once the urgency to perform spiritual masculinity had receded. Had he not remained bound to the template with a zealous new girlfriend to keep it up for, who might he have become? What freedom would he have discovered had he not become a twenty-one-year-old husband fourteen months later? By the time self-awareness dawned, it was too late. We'd walked an aisle and committed to the bit.

I have deep compassion for the man he thought he had to be, not unlike the support staff I thought I had to be. His social belonging was predicated on being the head; no other part would suffice. Most of this was a byproduct of our environment, some simply of function of youth. Had we given growing up a chance, we might have widened our gaze and picked a better-suited partner, a better-suited *life* that didn't chafe in the same wounded spots for twenty-six years.

I reject the patriarchal narrative that says this is how men should be, this is how women should be, and this is how power dynamics should be. I condemn it everywhere it reigns. It does not harm just the women but the men, not just the girls but the boys. It is the ruination of freedom. It robs us of autonomy and forces us into caricatures.

Patriarchy is a villain, and I grieve what it stole from both of us.

Ugh.

I absolutely wanted this book to be funnier.

Morning Jen and Night Jen

I spend a great deal of every therapy session on how to parent my kids through this upheaval. Notable instruction out there focuses on younger children, scripts suitable for second graders, kids going back and forth every weekend, shared custody, none of which I have. I have older kids who live here exclusively with developed emotions and full knowledge of the story. "Mommy and Daddy will always love you even though we aren't married anymore" won't pass muster.

"I think about the kids around the clock," I tell my counselor. "I really want to be a good mom right now. I want them to heal." I proceed to list my endless interventions and await my Therapy Award.

A fun note she gives is how codependency also derails parenting, and I might do a self-eval here. Am I trying to manage their emotions? Am I "making suggestions" on what they should do/say/think/feel? Am I making excuses for their dad's choices? Am I projecting toward some future outcome I want? Am I prioritizing instruction over connection? Coaching over comfort? Apparently they have to live their own stories, including the hard parts, and it isn't my job to fix any of it. I guess my job is just to bear witness and hold vigil with them. I don't pay her to boss me around, but alas.

"Jen, why don't you spend some energy mothering yourself?" she suggests.

First of all, her response to my parenting labor is underwhelming.

Second of all, I don't really get this. *All I do* is handle my adult shit. I make a list every morning and tick off tasks like I'm possessed. I have printed and scanned and notarized and submitted so much paperwork for so many things, I've ripped through three reams of paper. I am *killing* productivity, life management, financial solvency, and property oversight.

Wait, is that not what she meant by *mothering*?

The Enneagram 3 often confuses productivity with nurture; a completed task list is better than sex. But perhaps my therapist isn't suggesting that "scanning life insurance documents" equates to "gentle self-mothering." God, the amount of work it takes to exit my head and live in my body is colossal.

"So, like . . . mother myself as in . . . I want to say . . . " (Bless me.)

"Jen, what would a good mother do here?"

"Tell me to drink more water and quit Facebook stalking."

"Now you're getting somewhere."

So I audit my daily rhythms to assess what might feel like kindhearted parenting. Not like a teacher assigning benchmarks, not like a preacher dictating behaviors, not like a coach hyping the play call. But like a mother taking care of her beloved's little heart and body and feelings as if they matter more than the work rate.

Lo and behold, I find a couple of soft landing places. I institute Morning Jen and Night Jen (Day Jen is on the clock because a zebra can't change her stripes overnight). It goes something like this:

Night Jen is to be super, super sweet to Morning Jen. I don't ask much of her because Day Jen wears us all out.

1. She cleans the dinner dishes or makes sure a kid does it. When Morning Jen walks out to a clean kitchen with wiped-down counters, she wants to make out with Night Jen.
2. She gets the coffee ready and sets the timer. Morning Jen has

no greater joy than Texas Pecan brewing as her alarm goes off. *The happiness.*

3. Night Jen washes our face! This is such a nice thing to do! She lathers on all the potions and serums, and sets a large glass of ice water by the bed. Morning Jen loooooooves waking up with a clean, oiled face and lack of dehydration.

With this, Morning Jen wakes up fresh as a daisy and ready to serve Day Jen, who kicks almost all the ass percentage-wise, but only because Night Jen and Morning Jen came in so clutch:

1. Morning Jen gets up right away (no snooze) and immediately brushes her teeth. I realize this doesn't seem like it should make the cut, but sometimes it becomes eleven fifteen before teeth get brushed, and what good mother would allow that?? Day Jen deserves a mouth that doesn't taste like a sewer until lunchtime.

2. Morning Jen makes the bed and opens the blinds. My mom has made her bed every morning for fifty years. I've made my bed never. The *way* I feel with my bed beautifully made with the pillows arranged and the sheets crisp. All day long Day Jen is delighted to walk through this neat, sunshiny room. Look at me! Making my bed! I'm grown!

3. Because Night Jen was so true-blue, Morning Jen just pours herself some coffee, which is miraculously ready by the time she gets to the kitchen; lights her favorite candle (eucalyptus and lavender); and chooses the soothing morning playlist from Pandora because 2004 called and it can pry Pandora out of our dead hands. Alexa, play Ben Rector Pandora station. Play Civil Wars Pandora station. Play David Gray Pandora station.

And just like that, I am mothered. I feel tidy and centered and soothed. My bedroom is lovely, my face is "dewy" per Sydney's instruction (the youngs know about things), the house is giving full calm vibes, and Day Jen is ready to greet the teenagers with breakfast.

Sometimes nurture looks like clean countertops and 1% retinol face oil.

I absolutely love loving myself well.

I guess I am a good mom.

Women

It is 2000. I am twenty-six years old with a two-year-old and a newborn. We are entirely in the weeds. I had been teaching elementary school for four years until my daughter was born, and now at this point I don't make enough money to cover full-time childcare for two babies. The math is unambiguous, and I quit my job to raise the littles. There is not a single month we have enough money. We play a game every pay cycle called What Doesn't Get Paid? It is the least fun game on earth.

My husband is the latest hire at a church start-up in a fancy part of Austin. We convene in a high school fine arts facility, and that alone feels rogue and hip: "There are no rules in this house. We're not like a *regular* church. We're a *cool* church." The band plays radio songs on Sunday (but make it Jesus). Our first weekend on staff, the pastor shows a *Saturday Night Live* clip during the service. Everyone is stylish and youngish, and having only been in traditional Baptist churches my entire life, I'm obsessed.

We are the youth pastors, so we're always with the kids. Every teenager drives a nicer car than we do. We give a Realtor our budget and a zip code; she unironically shows us an abandoned home with no front door. Declining the squatter house, we recalibrate our desired location. Since we can't afford to live anywhere near the church, we buy a small house on the southernmost edge of town with a one-car garage and no bathroom on the first floor. We paint every interior square inch the color palette of the moment: plum, taupe, butterscotch, and one room red because we're here to *live*, dude. One morning, our neighbor's truck is on cinder blocks with stolen tires, but whatever because we have a red bedroom and little blond babies and our church band plays "Beautiful Day" by U2 on Sunday mornings.

My first Austin friend is Trina; her husband is also on the church staff. By default (as all wives are), she is in charge of "women's ministry" (unpaid). Ministry has always been sustainable through the two-for-one approach. She has never done this. Her career is in advertising, and Andrew was in the navy. Church planting in the 2000s is the Wild West. Trina goes in for the kill:

"Jen, you have to lead a small group for women."

"I certainly do not. I don't know anything about women. I'm scared of them."

"There aren't enough people here. No one is in charge."

"Trina, I already have to ride buses to youth camp. Can I live?"

"You know more than most of us. You have to teach."

"Dear God."

"He can't help you now."

Bullied into adult ministry and distinctly unqualified, I am assigned my first small group at a lavish house, and I am the leader. I'm nauseated with nerves. The other women outrank me in every way: age, money, sophistication. I am from Kansas. I have no practice with fancy Westlake people. I am a baby. I'm unskilled. I'm the wife.

To my sincere shock, I love it. I freaking love it. I love them, the women. I am stunned at the joy of being in a room full of grown-ups. What are these conversations?? Look at us thinking adult thoughts! This is stimulating and interesting and relevant to my actual world. Like I am physically possessed, some dormant leader inside me sparks to life. I forgot she was in there. I am not the student pastor's wife sleeping on the gym floor at a lock-in. Not the elementary teacher without an extra second of energy in a calendar day. My brain is activated and on fire with thrill.

That small group wraps up, and everything feels different. I am awake in a new way. I gather a group of fifteen women or so, and we start meeting every Thursday night at Christi's house for Bible study. It is my favorite two hours of every week. Because I don't relate to what's available, I write my own curriculum. I have no concept of format or craft, of course, but I count the minutes each night until I can put my babies to bed so I can start writing.

When my fingers touch that keyboard, something happens to me. Whole paragraphs come to me fully formed. Unexposed to Christian writing for women, I just write like I talk, and write how I learn, and write about serious things in a funny way because I don't know you can't do that. It is as if I've discovered a secret portal in my mind. Everything is vibrant. I watch myself write and lead and create and connect, and I think:

This.

Is.

It.

A new friend a few years older than me comes to our group. Loren is the kind of woman you want to immediately make yours. She has a saucy mouth and interesting ideas, and she slides right into the mix. We do our usual nonstop, two-hour discussion about what we are studying, which is currently the book of Isaiah (easy breezy! Prophetic anarchy!). I give Loren my info and demand she join our little crew for infinity. I get an email from her later that night:

"I like you. You're funny and smart. You have a power about you."

That's it. Short and sweet. I'm sure she just dashed it off, but I must read it a dozen times. I close it and reopen it. Lie there thinking about it, then read it again. I'm dazed by this casual observation. It is like I've never been given a compliment before. For whatever reason, this hits different. I don't know it yet, but I will never forget this exact moment.

Funny.

Smart.

Powerful.

What if I am?

Bono

The heart is a bloom,
Shoots up through the stony ground.

-U2, "Beautiful Day"

Internet

I haven't told the internet yet. It knows something is wrong, but if ever my little family craved privacy, it is surely now. Having a mom strangers love/hate/idealize/criticize pretty much sucks for the kids on the best of days, much less the worst, and we are certainly in the worst. The last thing they want is middle-aged women flooding their DMs trying to figure-out-what-happened-disguised-as-a-prayer.

I don't know what to do about any of it. My husband moved out a couple of months ago. I am AWOL on social media, the location of most of my work and community. I don't know how to talk about anything. What am I going to do, casually discuss back-to-school? Post a recipe? I stop working entirely. I can't fake it. I physically cannot pretend business is carrying on as usual. So I choose silence. Which doesn't go unnoticed.

Not only is our life dismantled, but I've talked publicly about marriage for fifteen years. This is such a catastrophic failure. My mind replays hundreds of paragraphs, chapters, pictures, and posts I've written about marriage, our marriage specifically; I posted one dreamy-looking picture of us the week before everything fell to shreds. I leave it up. I didn't know then. It was true to me that day.

I want to Bubble Wrap my little family and tuck us away from prying eyes forever. Please, God, just let my kids catch their fucking breath. Can we remain protected from public opinion long enough to grieve in private? Can we stay in our huddle like other broken families get to do? And share it with our community when we are ready?

A "journalist" whose website says "Reporting the truth. Restoring the church" (you decide if that sounds like neutral journalistic integrity) noses around my online silence, secures the public record of our filing, writes an article divulging our divorce, and discredits my leadership as a Christian. Embedded in the article is a boxed graphic: "Your tax-deductible gift helps our journalists report the truth and hold Christian leaders and organizations accountable."

She is a lightning rod for self-righteous fundamentalists. The comment feed immediately fills with people saying "So not surprised" and "She has always been about getting attention" and "It's a shame women followed her" and "Jen opened the door and let Satan in" and "Stop calling her a Christian." Every hateful word is directed at me; ironically, my husband is omitted from the reckoning. Within minutes, these same people skip over to my online spaces to gloat and condemn. It is an emotional bludgeoning.

My phone begins blowing up before 8:00 a.m. My name starts trending. She has told the world our private agony and put our family on display like circus animals paraded for entertainment. When widely criticized online, she shrugs it off and says that I am a leader held to a higher standard. I deserve this exposure. My children deserve nothing. We don't deserve privacy. We don't even deserve decency.

We haven't even told all our family.

Our story is yanked from our hands and broadcast by a self-proclaimed watchdog. This is all in the name of "faithfulness to the church," and for her, the cruelty creates no cognitive dissonance. As a half measure, she has the gall to message *my children.* Caleb, eighteen, must manage this woman in his DMs saying: "King [not bothering to get his name right], I didn't intend to hurt your family. I was just reporting." His subtle response: "Fuck all the way off."

And God help everyone in my actual circle fielding dozens of texts from everyone who ever barely knew them: Hey! Haven't talked in a while! Thinking about you! Also . . . is Jen okay? Soooo, what happened?

My kids pull their social accounts. My friends create an on-the-spot moratorium and stop answering their phones. Our church's answering machine fills up. My siblings go offline. My assistant freezes my website. We ghost every "request for comment." It is crushing.

But you know, the church needed "to be restored." This woman delivered her pound of flesh.

Simple

How did I get here? Seriously, how did Jen Hatmaker the Pastor's Wife and Faith Leader become a spiritual orphan from the church that raised me? I've interviewed hundreds of leading voices, spoken on countless stages, attended conference after conference. I have every tool at my disposal. Was I handed a defective enterprise? And in what ways did I participate in the sham?

Since I was a six pound, seven ounce baby born in Wichita, Kansas, I never met a rule I didn't love. Give me all the rules! Clear metrics for success! Which I will achieve or die trying. I just like things plain. I perfected the skill of condensing complex information to its innermost nesting doll early on. I like a rock-bottom premise: " . . . so the main takeaway is this." Now we know what to think, or do, or say, or believe.

Simple.

Organized religion was my perfect drug. Now, not "belief in mystery" or "connection to the divine" or any of those softer woo-woo versions, but rather church hierarchies, clear rules with clear consequences, reliable groupthink, outward criterion. This is what we believe: simple. This is what we do: simple. This is what we don't do: simple. This is what's true: simple.

I always understood God through my mind.

Wizard, give her a heart! It sounds horribly clinical, but my main motivation was faithfulness. While a fear-based urgency to please God wasn't a healthy impetus either, my spiritual worldview was to finally get (or figure out how to stay) on God's good side. I just wanted to do the right thing. Or maybe I didn't want to do the wrong thing. Either way, *right and wrong* composed my entire ideology. Thus a fairly rigid spiritual environment created safety for my worried, frantic little heart bullied into submission by my dominant mind.

The problem is that "simple" wouldn't hold up. That isn't how life is or how people are. Simple is an opiate for the mind, but it is a real shit show for the heart. And if you live long enough and pay attention at all, your heart refuses to stay silent after a while. The mind can be an uncomplicated mechanism but the heart has eyes.

My heart began seeing what my mind was simply reducing. Turns out, she was highly attuned to one primary signal: other people's pain. That was her frequency, and she refused to remain disengaged, no matter how much my mind attempted to abridge the data. Like pulling a stray thread of a poorly made sweater, once I tugged at the first strand, the whole damn thing started unraveling.

For me, it started with the poor. Up close, the tidy explanations of poverty, homelessness, and the American Dream absolutely stopped working. There was nothing simple about any of it. There were micro levels and macro levels, individual factors inside whole systems. There was no baseline explanation or solution. It was messy. It was disorienting.

The thread of poverty was adjacent to several others: refugees, mental illness, wage gaps, addiction. Those began unraveling quicker than I could even assimilate the talking points. Immediately following those threads came the lack of affordable housing, childcare, insurance, transportation. The dead-last word I would use to describe any of these issues is *simple*. My straightforward thesis where "doing the right thing = guaranteed outcomes" was falling apart.

The cozy sweater I'd wrapped around my entire life was half in tatters.

Which brought me to two threads that would ultimately undo my life, my career, and my simple way of understanding the world forever. For now, just the first:

Racism.

White supremacy was a concept I had zero exposure to in my assigned/chosen homogeneous environments. But once you nose around the rubble of injustice, racism emerges instantly. It is, simply, everywhere. It is fundamentally dispersed through the air filters. Racism was the bedrock of the American origin story and has remained a scourge on our culture at every level, in every system, throughout every generation.

Because the threads of disenfranchisement are all connected, the homeless community was my first experience of racial bias in the criminal justice system. I could write fifty million words here, but the rock-bottom premise is this (*let me have it*): Black people are no more criminal than white people in any category; they are just suspected, arrested, charged, and punished more. No credible data suggests otherwise. The numbers are outrageous and irrefutable.

This learning curve for me was so steep, I shudder to recall *anything* I said or asked back then (Jesus, be a muzzle). But unlike the denial of racism, which breaks down instantly, my heart led where my mind could sustain, because Black pain is so acute, such a clarion call, only the gravest fool would say: "The entire Black community is wrong." Their suffering captured me, then the facts converted me.

What is *right* should also be what is *true*.

And here I began experiencing a shocking disconnect from the online faith community I was leading. I did not see this train wreck coming, because what is right should also be what is true, and I thought we agreed on this. There could not be a higher premium placed on "truth" inside evangelicalism. It was the engine behind every doctrine, every position. Certainly, sometimes right and true things were also hard (loving your enemies, patience, and humility come to mind), but Jesus mentioned the "count the cost" clause. Once we knew something was true, *particularly* when associated with disenfranchised people, the right thing to do was obvious.

Imagine my surprise when I began discussing white supremacy, and tons of my Christian followers lost their shit. I mean, lost it. My comment feed was a daily nightmare. I lost a thousand followers a day. Condemning racism threw white evangelical women into a rage. It was like I'd been leading a den of lions and they turned on me once I changed their preferred diet.

I kept thinking I wasn't explaining the data well, since what is right is also what is true, so I must not have been presenting the facts correctly; otherwise we would be in obvious alignment here. Justice is in our Christian wheelhouse! This is, like, supposed to be our thing. I didn't save my coins for Lottie Moon for nothing, dammit. I know how we were raised.

Since I couldn't convincingly make the case, I put Black leader after Black activist after Black pastor after Black businesswoman after Black author in front of my community. Now we'd start cooking with gas. Of course I bungled the original message; what did I know? I was a white girl from Kansas. Let the experts do a better job here and rally the troops. They brought not only clear data but also their lived experiences, the most compelling stories of all.

This was when I learned that "what is true" mostly factors in when it benefits white, straight Christians. If it doesn't, or more to the point, if it threatens the narrative, it will be instantly divorced from "what is right" and rebranded. White supremacy, regardless of how documented, regardless of how personally explained, regardless of how *true*, challenged inherent bias and the white Christian obsession with appearing virtuous. It disabused the fantasy that opportunity is earned on merit in a color-blind culture that operates in equality. Huge swaths of my community were combative toward the Black voices I promoted and downright hostile with me before joining the mass exodus.

It was disorienting, startling, and . . . eye-opening.

Because if white evangelicalism was willing to say racism is obsolete when plain evidence exists to the contrary, if what is true no longer matters for what is right, what else might they be wrong about?

This would ultimately lead me to the second thread.

Another Word About That

In the continuing "how did I get here" postmortem, I find myself examining the doctrinal position where the heart and mind are out of alignment, where cognitive dissonance is a spiritual cross to bear. I was raised to not only accept that tension but trust it.

Example: Probably the thing you want to do the very least that would be hard and lonely and take you away from the normal dreams you have as a human is the ultimate Christian thing to do. Faithfulness of the highest order. (See: missionaries.)

Example: Shaming LGBTQIA+ people, forcing them into conversion therapy, banishing them to permanent celibacy, and kicking them out of their families and churches is just "the cost of sin." We are sorry they are committing suicide at seven times the average rate but they shouldn't have been gay. These are just the biblical rules.

Example: Regardless of their gifts, natural leadership capacity, brilliance, or innate power, women are to spiritually and socially submit to men as their pastors, thought leaders, and spouses. Men automatically have authority, because the Bible says.

We were told these were right, but they felt terrible. We were instructed to discredit the catastrophic outcomes: colonization, suicide, broken families, broken hearts, broken bodies, subjugation, abuse, corruption, dehumanization, the loss of personhood. The fruit of these trees was rotten. Not one bad apple, not one questionable limb; rotten to the roots.

But believe what you are told, not what you see.

Believe what you are taught, not what you feel.

Believe what we say, not what you know deep in your soul.

Why were we asked to accept such misalignment between our head and heart? Why did that dissonance make something *right* instead of flagged for *wrong*? Why was the heart branded as so untrustworthy, particularly when it was grieved by human suffering?

Who benefits when we are required to overlook red flags and blindly follow?

Who loses?

I wonder if identifying the winners and losers tells us something important.

A Concern

It is a complex endeavor to examine the various systems that encouraged teenagers to get married, defer to men, distrust their bodies, and diminish their own gifts. What kind of ground allows for such shallow roots? Some combination of patriarchy plus religion, gender roles plus groupthink, power plus the threat of exclusion became the soil in which my marriage ultimately died.

Trying to lay the axe at the root of the rotten tree is complicated, important work.

But in doing so here, I worry about the one-dimensionality. Separating individual people from the systems is tricky pruning. Institutionally, we have men in leadership, shame-based purity requirements, limited agency for women, a deeply punitive cancel culture. This operates exactly as intended. It is highly functional as long as women don't challenge it or leave.

But individually, these systems include some of the best people I know. My own mom and dad were insiders most of my life, and if I could choose any parents on God's earth, I'd pick them. Hazel, the church bookkeeper who loved me with limitless attention and candy. Mrs. Ruby, the world's most elegant pastor's wife, who treasured us. As adults, Steve and Norma, John and Mary, Terry and Rebecca, Gary and Claudia: parents of our students who loved us, genuinely, like their own kids. They were family. To say nothing of my own best friends, every last one a derivative of church, Baptist college, or Christian-ish writing.

So many people gathered under these problematic umbrellas are, to put it succinctly, my beloveds.

How do I reject the systems without disparaging the people I love?

Resistance

I was raised by a mother who is something of an . . . under-responder. I didn't even know moms regularly worried about, well, anything. My mom's motto was basically "It'll be fine." She didn't "over" much: over-react, overprotect, overrule, overkill, overcorrect, overbear. I asked her once when my kids were little, "Mom? Did you and your friends worry you were doing everything wrong when we were kids?" And she famously responded, "God, no. You and your friends 'parent' [air quotes employed]. We just raised you." Welp.

Reader, you are forbidden to interpret this as criticism. My mom was the only calm human being in our house. While the rest of us ran up and down the scales with our hair on fire, the embodiment of melo-drama, Mom held a steady note that never faltered. So rather than an entire family in the rafters, Mom nonchalantly filed her nails, waiting for us to descend from whatever ceiling we were glued to that day.

However, because she was unflappable and under-responded to things that should have arguably raised at least an eyebrow, we had no idea we were supposed to be afraid of stuff. I could fill fifty books with things I have absolutely no fear of *that I should*. No hint of a lie, I did not own a key to my own house for a solid decade. "What if someone breaks in??" gasped friends. "Who on earth would break in??" replied Jen, truly baffled. Against substantial evidence, I have steadfastly be-lieved no one means any harm, people won't lie, nothing will go wrong, and everything is safe. I live in the upper portion of the top half of the glass. (This is no exaggeration. Ask anyone who loves me.)

So it is genuinely disorienting to lose my marriage and discover I am now afraid of *everything*. Despite the face creams and bedside ice water, I barely sleep fifteen seconds between 2:30 and 4:30 a.m. for months, my mind a cauldron of panic. I'm no longer afraid of a break-in but a breakdown. It would be quicker to list the things I am *not* afraid of than outline everything that feels ravaged. Dread wraps its tentacles, and I am certain I will never feel internally safe again.

I am afraid I might die of pain. I am afraid I might live with pain. I am afraid I can't do it on my own. I am afraid for my kids. I am afraid for our future. I am afraid about money. I am afraid about my career, my community, my church, our friends, bills, yard maintenance, our cars, my in-laws, my unborn grandbabies, loneliness, being broken, my credibility, faith, college, retirement, trauma, holidays, my own patterns, my foolishness, my naivete, my ignorance.

I guess I should have been afraid all along.

Which is the exact sentiment I take into therapy: *I'm scared now. There is reason to be scared. I should have been scared. I will always be scared. Please teach me how to live as a scared person for the rest of my days. I have no training.*

As you might surmise, my therapist thinks this approach to the next forty years is ill-conceived. She asks me horrific questions like "What are you exactly afraid of?" And I am like, "Ma'am, this session is $125 an hour. I will get to the end of the list and owe you a quarter of a million dollars." But because I am an Enneagram Three and want to win therapy, I list my fears and beg her to tell me how to make it stop. I want none of it. I want to sleep through the night. I want to feel my old sense of confidence for fifteen minutes a day. I want this in my rear-view mirror and need the therapist's secret formula for making bad things end.

"Jen, there is how you feel, then there is your resistance to how you feel. The first is hard. The second is catastrophic. You are afraid right now, which is appropriate, because you are a human who experienced trauma. This is a normal response. But your refusal to face your fears will delay your healing more than any other factor. Your fear isn't the problem. Your resistance to fear is."

I don't prefer this. My $125 an hour is meant to evade the suffering and resurrect the sparkling person who doesn't own a house key. *All I do* is resist my fears. At no point do I sit with my feelings and just let them exist. I fight like a wildcat against every worry, every doubt, every possibility of future anguish. I argue with my terror, give myself Girl Boss lectures, seize any sixty-second burst of optimism and declare myself "healed." I resist fear like it is my paying job.

Only because I can't tolerate the suffering anymore, I try to figure out what my therapist is saying. I genuinely have no practice with this. I am a shiny girl born to a shiny dad with a zen mom and a historical nonchalance toward fear. In a sentence that costs me $2.08, I say to my therapist: "Talk to me like a kindergartener. When you say 'stop resisting your fear,' what that means is . . . that I would . . . I think the thing is . . . just decide to be happy?" (I am definitely not winning therapy, and this is why counselors need their own counselors.)

With a barely concealed sigh, she explains the rudimentary practices to embrace fear instead of resist it: Go soft when a fear rises up, unclench, relax my forehead and hands and shoulders. I learn to breathe in for eight seconds, hold for four, then exhale slowly for another eight, and I'll be damned if *breathing* doesn't help calm the internal panic. What on earth? Even babies know how to breathe! And they didn't even have to pay to learn!

I am learning to let a scary thought ride its own wave without trying to deny it; I just let it live in my scared little mind while breathing helps me endure it. I tell myself: "It's okay that you feel scared about this. It is a normal way to feel. You're not doing something wrong. Relax your forehead. Check if your hands are clenched." Lo and behold, the thought finds its end and I don't die from it.

It doesn't make sense, but facing a fear, letting it be what it is, letting myself feel how I feel, while intentionally staying calm and keeping my body soft is better than resisting. I don't know how it works. Resisting fear seems smarter. It seems like kickass, Annie Oakley, mind-over-matter shit, and I can promise I'd still be doing that if it worked. I'd be sparring against scary thoughts and terrifying what-ifs, talking myself out of every emotion. But some transmutation happens when I let the fear rise, peak, and recede without a fight. It forfeits a great deal of its power, like it feeds off the strain, and without the tension, it goes slack.

Whatever I am resisting finds a quicker end when I let it exhaust its energy without my participation. I am learning to just let it come, knowing it will also go. I practice shifting my attention to my forehead, my hands, my shoulders, and my breath. Most of my fear is not productive anyway—wild inventions that are uncontrollable, unchangeable, or unlikely. My guess is that almost zero percent of them will come to pass. Well, to be fair, who knows if my unborn grandbabies will make bad choices because of my divorce? I'll let you know later if I should have hung on to that one.

I'm developing some tolerance for fear when it comes. I'm learning to shrink its run time, and that's about the best we can do, I guess. The less oxygen I give it with resistance, the quicker it moves through. Maybe one day I'll return to the bottom portion of the top half of the glass; too soon to say.

Although on my best, most regulated day, I will *never* under-respond like my mom, who, upon learning my brother drove her Jeep into a river, shrugged and said: "Well, it's just a car." Jesus, give me one-tenth the restraint of Jana King, but so help me, if one of my sons drives my Bronco into a river, I will have to forfeit my salvation. Hello, rafters, my old friend.

The Article

And now, the second thread.

It is 2016 and the world is on fire. Collectively, we are processing the on-the-spot murders of Alton Sterling and Philando Castile by law enforcement; we haven't recovered from Eric Garner, Ferguson, Tamir Rice. The unhinged TV personality Donald Trump is running for president, and everything seems cartoonish, a dark rendering of reality.

I am in the weeds online every day. I simply cannot stay silent. I am both anti–systemic racism and anti-Trump as my only feasible paths. I thought what is right stemmed from what is true, and I am not yet unseated from that naivete. But these two positions place me in direct opposition to a great deal of my community, and the environment is openly hostile.

October 25, fourteen days before the election, I give an interview to Religion News Service. It is supposed to cover the speaking tour I'm currently on, but it very quickly becomes a litmus test for conservative talking points. I fail them in rapid fire:

"Are you still a conservative?"

"Why are you bothered by Donald Trump?"

"Are you going to vote for Hillary?"

"Where do you stand on abortion?"

"What are your thoughts on Black Lives Matter?"

In ten minutes flat, I speak in blunt terms about complex issues,

issues I generally handle with thought and care and nuance. It is scorched earth. A background reel starts quietly running in my mind: *You will pay for this*.

And then:

"Do you support gay marriage? Do you think an LGBT relationship can be holy?"

I'm not new here. I've watched prominent evangelicals reverse their position not just on gay marriage, reasonably supported from a civic standpoint, but also toward the theological position that gay people should be fully affirmed at every level of personhood, church, and society. The punishment is predictable and relentless. While other hot-button issues cause a disturbance, this one is the death knell.

"I do. I would officiate a gay wedding with gladness and I would drink champagne."

I am canceled immediately. My publisher disavows me in a press release the next day. My books are pulled off shelves and, in the case of my most successful book, put out of print. I am released from every speaking event on my calendar. My social media following is halved in two hours. My tour team is bombarded with patrons demanding a refund. A new article is released once an hour:

"The High Cost of Popular Evangelical Jen Hatmaker's Gay Marriage Comments" (*The Washington Post*)

"This Evangelical Leader Denounced Trump. Then the Death Threats Started" (*Politico*)

"Jen Hatmaker on White Christian Women and Politics" (*The Atlantic*)

"Hatmaker Heresy" (*The American Conservative*)

"Jen Hatmaker Affirms Gay Marriage – Proves She Has No Idea Who God Is" (*Pulpit & Pen*)

"The Theological Mess in the Moxie of Jen Hatmaker" (Christian Research Institute)

"Pastors, It's Time to Audit What Your Women Are Studying" (Berean Research)

These are endless. A few famous-y friends speak against me to create separation and protect their own brands. Others try valiantly to hold the relational line but it won't keep. Someone leaves a pile of burned books in my front yard. My husband's latest book on church leadership is three months old and now dead in the water. The evangelical community does what it does when it comes to dissenters:

Terrorizes and expels.

I get very still, very quiet. There is no way to fight the mob, only endure it. This moment was coming, and I am almost relieved it is here. My good standing has been in peril for anyone paying attention. At this moment, I can choose my career, or I can choose my integrity, but I cannot have both. Salvaging my insider status would be at the expense of my convictions and the communities they represent, the coward's fictional middle ground. My days of silence for this community are over, and it is to my shame it took me so long. With terror and relief, I plunge from the tightrope I'd been walking.

I free-fall.

When something finally catches me, we'll see if I have anything left.

First "Christmas"

At the three-month mark, I've emerged from shocked paralysis and am fully overfunctioning. I feel it but cannot stop, because overworking is my natural homeostasis. I haven't returned to work but am applying this hyperfocus to getting my personal shit together. Frankly, there is so much to do, I'm grateful my capacity is apparently able to expand beyond any sane level.

Refinance the house: check.

Set up all new bank accounts: check.

Transfer all bills to my name only: check.

Handle the entire legal divorce alone: check.

Manage the lawyer: check.

Get current on taxes: check.

Hire a bookkeeper: check.

Sort out health insurance: check.

Figure out the kids' tuition, rent, etc.: check.

Oversee all virtual COVID school: check-ish.

This list goes on and on. The kids are with me full-time. Gavin has moved home temporarily because managing a ranch in Alabama while his family imploded proved too lonely. So four of the five kids are here—two in high school, and two in triage. Frankly, we are all in triage.

Interestingly, despite the swirl of loss and number of children, the house is peaceful. Very, very peaceful. I notice instantly. The triggered, explosive energy moved out and with it went the majority of conflict. We talk in normal tones. We don't erupt on one another. Miraculously, we laugh a lot. You don't realize you aren't walking on eggshells anymore until you can't hear them crunching under your feet.

We are approaching the first holiday season without an intact family. I don't even know how to feel. Our traditions are as deep as the ocean. We have *things*. At this time, I am the only functioning parent. This is all on me. Everything is. I have to figure out how to fill this house with joy, dammit. Something, anything, needs to feel cozy.

I turn to my overproducing side and ask, "What would you do?"

She says: "Put up the Christmas tree in October."

"Brilliant."

So on October 9, out come the Christmas boxes. Up go the lights. Out pop the Nativities. Thanks to the miracle of streaming television, on go the Hallmark Christmas movies. The red plaid Christmas pillows adorn the couch. Six instead of seven stockings deck the mantel. "Alexa, play Christmas classics." Advent candles are arranged on the dining table. We decorate the Christmas tree and reenact the requisite scene from *Christmas Vacation* when we flip the lights on: "Joy to the wooooooooorld . . ."

It is ninety-one degrees outside.

We cackle at the absurdity as we toast our mugs of hot cocoa.

Why can't we engineer wild, grand gestures to shoehorn joy into sad places? Why shouldn't we put up Christmas early or paint a room hot pink or string twinkle lights across our dining table? For that matter, sometimes the only obvious thing to do is dye your hair platinum or start wearing outrageous glasses or serve your family cake for breakfast. When all else fails, pull your kids out of school and go see a movie at twelve thirty in the afternoon and let everyone drink full-sugar Coke.

It is saying: "We didn't choose that, but we can choose this. We didn't want that, but there is no reason we can't have this." Life may steal some happiness but it can't confiscate joy, or at least not all of it. We still contain outrageousness, and we ought to use it because it is fun, and fun is underrated when you're sad. At some point, we are exhausted from suffering and just want to watch *Christmas at Honeysuckle Lane* wearing Santa pajamas in October.

That night alone in my living room with the Christmas tree lit and Halloween commercials on, I think about my beloveds tucked into their rooms all around me, safe and loved, warm and fed, at least temporarily delighted and entertained, and I realize not everything happens *to* us. Sometimes, despite it all, we decide to make magic happen.

Gurney

I've obviously pulled myself out of the teaching rotation at church. I preach on Sunday mornings several times a year. Like the rest of religious America, we've been streaming services online since March. I haven't faced church folk yet. Unless they are interested in a twenty-five-minute sermon showcasing an emotional breakdown, best I stay out of the fray for now.

My friends Brett and Matthew are getting married at our little church. They are the dearest beings that ever lived. Because COVID is a thief of ordinary joy, the in-love-and-engaged population has either delayed or pivoted their wedding plans. Brett and Matthew arrange a virtually streamed ceremony with ten people socially distanced in our church.

I watch from my porch swing, *engorged with enchantment.*

That's it. I believe! I believe instantly in love, I believe in hope, shit, I believe in marriage. Everything is beautiful. Young gay men can get married in church! At my church at least! Love is real. Weddings are perfect. Futures are secure. Look at these darling souls committing their lives to each other. They are stunning. Our church is a safe place. These are my people. I feel positively renewed. Everything's gonna be all right, rockabye.

With my lashes still wet with happy tears, I text our lead pastor

Jason: I'm ready for the pulpit. Put me back in. My epiphany is complete. I made it. It is Friday.

Monday I am hit with such a severe wave of despair, I can't get out of bed. I'm sunk. Grief is unquantifiable and nonlinear. I cannot work out the algorithm. Just like that, I feel small again. The heightened optimism evaporates, and I only feel the emptiness of loss.

In therapy that day, the pendulum swings to the opposite side entirely. I tell my counselor I can't do any of this. That I'm not capable, I can't handle all the responsibility alone, I am scared and worried and too far out of my depth. I thought I had it, but I don't. From Friday to Monday, the fall was great.

I text Jason: I am so sorry. I overshot. I'm not ready. I was only ready for that one hour and someone should have taken my phone away. It's too soon.

This is what he texts back:

Jen, nobody gets to push or pull or tug you anywhere. You get to do what you are able, engage what heals you, speak into only the things that bring you life. No one needs any more than that. You're still on the gurney, and that's perfectly fine. Time is what is needed. You will rise. Optimism might only come in small bursts right now, and that's okay. There's no shame in that. New life is coming, and we can wait.

My mom, an accomplished master gardener, told me: You can't tug on spring shoots of new plants. You have to wait. They are setting deep roots. You can't grow a crop by pulling on leaves and stalks. You just create the right conditions . . . and you wait.

I ponder my tendency to overidentify with the emotional extremes. Experiencing a high day doesn't mean the pain is over. Experiencing a low day doesn't mean the recovery is doomed. But living on the sliding scale is terribly disruptive; I'd rather camp in one of the poles and sim-ply declare *this is who I am now* and be done with it. I crave consistency.

But like Rilke wrote: "Let everything happen to you: beauty and terror. Just keep going. No feeling is final." Somehow I must hold on to both my pain and my hope; they each deserve my belief. They are both real, and they both matter.

I am on the gurney. I am underground. I am pushing toward the light. I am developing roots no one can see. I am waiting on spring shoots. I am still in winter.

I am all of these things, but none of them last.

Tomorrow will be different from today.

So I'll just keep fucking going.

Anniversary

December 29. Tomorrow would have been my twenty-seventh anniversary.

Last year on this day, I was positive that in twenty-four more years, I'd stand at the summit of a gorgeous fifty-year marriage, just like my in-laws, who celebrated last summer, and my parents, who will celebrate theirs in June. We come from a long line of Forever Marriages. We were gearing up for the much-deserved second half: sons- and daughters-in-law, grandbabies, travel, adventure. I had all my chips on us.

In my outermost imagination, I could not have envisioned finishing this year divorced. It catches me by surprise several times a day and shocks me anew. I can barely say the words *divorced* or *ex* or *single* without wondering who on earth I am talking about. I wear them like the most ill-fitting coat. These were never, ever, ever meant to be mine.

However, I find myself reaching for reflection on my first single December 30 since 1993. Regret doesn't make sense to me. What if I had chosen differently? What did I forfeit? Who would I be? What if I didn't marry him at nineteen? This line of thinking is a nonstarter, because everything I love most on earth is because I did. Imagining a different life would be at the expense of the one I cherish. Somehow I am able to hold two competing emotions: compassion for the teenagers who missed an independent young adulthood, and immense gratitude for everything that young marriage gave me. The losses are easy to catalog, but here are the wins after twenty-six years of marriage:

Five beautiful, spectacular kids. Irreplaceable. There is no them without who we were.

In-laws and a second family that will always be mine, where we will always belong, where we will always be loved.

Memories. No one can take them. No one can ruin them by whispering the future or suggesting they weren't real. They are safe and true and mine.

Myself. I have my whole, good, worthy self that I will protect for the rest of my days. My chips are now all on me.

And of course I have my family, my best friends, work that I love with my whole being. I guess some things are forever outside of marriage. I see my forever people. I see my forever community. I guess that means I see my forever. It's not incomplete after all.

So tomorrow, instead of wallowing, I am whisking Sydney and Remy to New York, and I will celebrate these breathtaking girls and being their mom. New memories, not old ones. The day will be not ruined but redeemed.

My forever looks different than I expected, but sometimes beautiful things do.

Shauna

The next day, I am in New York with my daughters thanks to a lovely, generous friend who texted: Would you like to stay in our apartment in NYC after Christmas? Would that feel healing? It is all yours.

The city is bizarre. Makeshift outdoor stalls with sketchy heaters are the only dining options. This normally bustling time is void of tourists. People visibly wear their exhaustion; tired faces abound. The city, if you can even imagine, feels quiet. New York suffered greatly during COVID. We all did. God, 2020 was the worst year of my life. May it burn in all our hells.

I call my friend Shauna, who lives in Chelsea. We meet bundled up in an outdoor kiosk for Italian food and tears. No one outside my Texas pod has seen me since my life fell apart. We order a bottle of wine and overreact to the plate of homemade focaccia and herbed oil. Thank heavens there is still bread and wine.

The server leaves the table; I take a deep breath and begin. I am noticeably unpracticed at telling this terrible story. I use a lot of words, a lot of tears. I'm all over the place. Shauna and I have been dear friends for fifteen years. I default to our history and don't mitigate the verbal deluge. We've been through plenty together. I know she can sift.

When I come up for air having rambled and emoted egregiously, Shauna leans back and hands me the most shocking observation. Not

"You'll get through this" or "I hate to see you this tortured" or "It won't always feel this way." She looks at me discerningly and says:

"I am relieved to see that you are still exactly you. You sound like you. You look like you. You're not broken."

I am stunned.

I wouldn't accept this pronouncement from most. Only a few people on earth really know me. Some know me a little. Some know a side of me. Some know a younger version of me. Some know me in a particular context. Some know only what I show them. Some know the internet me.

But Shauna knows me. If she thinks I am still me, then I must really still be me.

She sees me whole. This assessment alters something in my soul. I didn't know I was. I thought my husband's desertion stole precious pieces of me, that I was fragile and incomplete. I assumed I would never be the same, that everyone's experience of me would never be the same; a bottle of wine left uncorked too long, once lovely but disappointingly soured.

This trustworthy perception is a gift. It isn't aspirational, Shauna hasn't pinned some future version of me to the board. It isn't predicated on the terrifying hope that maybe one day I'll recover myself. She doesn't suggest that more healing or more counseling or more time or more work will patch my shattered soul together for some brittle version of who I once was.

I am still me, right now, right here, right in the thick of it.

My marriage is broken, but I'm not.

I guess no one can ever take me from me.

I stare at Shauna silently for ten seconds, then throw my head back and laugh with full-throated gratitude.

Here I still am.

Twinge

It isn't a particularly memorable day, in fact in hindsight I can't even pinpoint the year, but sometime during the melee of career building and raising kids, I stumble on an article about the greatest predictors of divorce. I'm not searching this out and certainly not self-assessing, but it crosses my desk and I take mild notice:

1. Criticism
2. Defensiveness
3. Stonewalling
4. Contempt

And I feel . . . a twinge.

Starbucks

In March 2011, my husband and I walk into a restaurant in Addis Ababa, Ethiopia, to meet the other adoptive parents in our travel group. We are all jetlagged, bundles of exposed nerves. We've been in the grueling process of international adoption for so very long and all have pictures and videos of the children we are about to finally meet. We are internet friends through the shared experience of home studies, caseworkers, court approvals, and anguish.

Of the ten couples in our travel group, eight are adopting babies. Only two are adopting older kids:

Ours are eight and five.

Susan and Ed are adopting three siblings: thirteen, five, and two.

While the baby parents sit serenely on blankets under trees with their tiny, immovable infants, the four of us are lightning rods for all the big kids at the orphanage. It is nonstop soccer, piggyback rides, fingernail painting, and card games. We push swings, sing songs, join dance parties. All four of us are sweat factories. We deliver gifts from other waiting families back home and take one million pictures, then promptly surrender our iPhones to preteen Ethiopian hands. We fall in love with our children, Ed and Susan's children, and each other.

Once home, the baby parents figure out nap schedules and we jump into elementary and middle school teacher conferences. Susan and I build a friendship long past the paperwork years and into our "big kids" actually becoming big.

Fast forward to 2020. My family has unraveled for the whole world to see. Only a few friends understand the grief of parenting adopted children through their second family disruption. When all I ever wanted was to give them permanency, loss doubled down on them. God, it is so spectacularly unfair.

The first Monday after our broken family became a known quantity, I get a text:

Susan has sent you a $25 gift card to Starbucks. Click here to redeem!

The next Monday, $25 to Starbucks.

The next Monday.

The next Monday.

The next Monday.

Susan sends me a Starbucks gift card every single Monday for six months.

Much is made about what to do when a friend is in crisis. What to say. What not to say. What to offer. What to send. What to text. The Monday Starbucks Ministry suggests it is not so much the thing as the love. The "I am still here" and "I care about your broken heart" and "I am thinking about you because weekends are full but Mondays are lonely."

Turns out no one can fix a husband who left his life. But you can certainly provide six months of soy vanilla lattes and, primarily and most importantly, your steady friendship week after week after grueling, hard week. Long past the typical expiration date of someone else's grief.

I consolidate most of it into one loaded gift card and give it to my youngest, most tender Ethiopian obsessed with Starbucks, whose first year of high school is worse than ever imagined.

"Who is all this from, Mom?"

"Joshua and Ruth and Dibora's mom."

"Oh, she must really love us."

Mrs. Palmer

I am a junior in high school. Mrs. Palmer is my AP English teacher. She has been putting up with high school bullshit for a really long time; I can't tell how old she is because all teachers in 1990 seem old. She keeps her gray hair cropped and stylish and dresses impeccably despite trying to inspire sluggish, blue-collar teens at Campus High School. Her signature move is a wearing a wide statement belt cinched around her tiny waist, as if Diane Keaton took a wrong turn somewhere and ended up in a cinder block classroom in Haysville, Kansas.

Our first unit is poetry, and perhaps no group of humans is less interested in composed literature than this room of sixteen-year-olds. Mrs. Palmer is Beethoven playing to screech owls. Telly Craig writes a poem about testicles and reads it with a straight face. Matt Belew sprawls across his desk and sleeps through every single class. David Mitchell refuses to bring his English book because he tells Mrs. Palmer "he is never going to open it." I am horrified. If she makes one penny less than a million dollars a year, it is not enough.

English is a high school requirement, of course, but I am most definitely a science girl. I am fascinated with anatomy and plan to study physical therapy. I have a brain for STEM; my favorite subjects are knowable, quantifiable, analytical, factual. I process truth through my mind. I am moved by research. Even as I love reading, my favorite part of the library is the card catalog. I immerse in algebra, physiology, calculus, biology and think: "This all makes sense." Though English is not my focus, I'm here to get an A, the same mission I've had since kindergarten.

Mrs. Palmer is doing her damnedest to expose us to beautiful poetry. We examine forms: stanza, rhyme, free verse, sonnets. We search for meaning and sort through allegory. Maybe 12 percent of the class is with her on any given day. I apply logic to poetry analysis and come up woefully short. I am stunned by my inability to crack the poetry code. I get one of my only C's ever on an essay breaking down "A Dream Within a Dream" by Poe; I parse it out into separate literary elements less like an artist and more like a robot. The structural semiotics I understand; the layered meaning misses me entirely.

I can't get poetry to make sense.

One day, fighting over the din of high school nonsense, Mrs. Palmer starts talking about her dad. It is weird to think of her having a dad. She is like a great-grandma or something. She almost isn't with us as she talks about what he meant to her, what kind of a father he was, what she remembers. Teachers don't talk to us like this, so the class slowly quiets down; even teenage assholes can occasionally read a room.

After a long pause, Mrs. Palmer says: "Poetry has always meant so much to me. My dad was my favorite person. When he got really sick, I couldn't bear living in this world without him. I read a poem to him on his deathbed. I think . . . I'll read it to you now."

Holy shit. The room goes silent. We are well beyond verse or form or critique. Even Matt is awake. I am sitting in the far right row three desks back. The air-conditioning is the only sound in the room. No one is moving a muscle. It feels like a full minute passes in silence before Mrs. Palmer takes a deep breath and begins:

"'Do Not Go Gentle into That Good Night' by Dylan Thomas.

Do not go gentle into that good night,
Old age should burn and rave at close of day;
Rage, rage against the dying of the light.

Though wise men at their end know dark is right,
Because their words had forked no lightning they
Do not go gentle into that good night.

Good men, the last wave by, crying how bright
Their frail deeds might have danced in a green bay,
Rage, rage against the dying of the light.

Wild men who caught and sang the sun in flight,
And learn, too late, they grieved it on its way,
Do not go gentle into that good night.

Grave men, near death, who see with blinding sight
Blind eyes could blaze like meteors and be gay,
Rage, rage against the dying of the light."

Mrs. Palmer pauses. We are glued to her, transfixed by these wise, good, wild, grave men who don't want to die. And in front of our eyes, our teacher wipes a tear and, in a shaky voice, reads the last verse:

"And you, my father, there on the sad height,
Curse, bless, me now with your fierce tears, I pray.
Do not go gentle into that good night.
Rage, rage against the dying of the light."

I am flattened. I can't breathe. Like I left my body and just returned to it, I feel tears dripping off my chin. I didn't even know I was crying.

I have to cover my mouth with my hand to stifle sobs. I am there with Mrs. Palmer at her father's bedside. I am urging him to fight for his life with her. I can see him fading and see her begging, and I want so desperately for him to rage against the dying of the light.

The combination of this poem and her reading of it cracks my heart open and something falls inside. These words have rearranged me. Some Welsh man wrote a poem in 1947 in Florence, my teacher read it to her dying father in the 1980s in Kansas, and now she has given it to us in 1990. I've gone somewhere new. I will never unknow this. Mrs. Palmer has changed my life in under ten minutes; I don't quite get how but I know she has.

Leaving class a few minutes later, I act against every teenage instinct: I stop by Mrs. Palmer's desk and throw my arms around her. I can't say anything. I can't even let go. I've lost all propriety. She of course saw me wiping my face earlier, pretending not to be coming undone in the middle of second period. She holds my face gently between her hands and says:

"Jennifer, words have always mattered. You have a gift for them. Use it."

Exactly three years later, I am married.

Another Poem I Love

"Bride"

How long have I been wed
to myself? Calling myself

darling, dressing for my own
pleasure, each morning

choosing perfume to turn
me on? How long have I been

alone in this house but not
alone? Married less

to the man than to the woman
silvering with the mirror.

I know the kind of wife
I need and I become her:

the one who will leave
this earth at the same instant

. . .

I do. I am my own bride,
lifting the veil to see

my face. Darling, I say,
I have waited for you all my life.

~*Maggie Smith*

One More Poem I Love

"I Am Not Your Cup of Tea"

I am not your cup of tea
because I am made too strong
and frankly, too hot
for you to enjoy
maybe you can tolerate me
in tiny sips but I don't want
to be tolerated. I want to be
devoured by those who value
all I am and who do not wish
I was in any way watered down
to meet your tepid tastes.

-David Gate*

*https://www.davidgatepoet.com/store/p/brqlor8xl86o62qqhorlonpi4pbtvo

Mexico

January 2021. My best friends and sister send a text: We are taking you to Mexico. You don't have to do anything but pack swimsuits and cutoffs.

I do not know where we are going, and I don't care. Parenting two high schoolers alone through COVID school has kicked our asses so badly, I am certain we will never recover. There is not nor will there ever be shared custody, so I am the sole parent during the fucking worst year ever. The kids are capsizing. I, pleasantly, have become a manic involuntary homeschool mom contributing to the dumbing down of America with a helpful rage/rebound/renounce cycle:

"I am absolutely done worrying about your grades. Either *you* worry about them or you fail. I already finished ninth grade in 1989."

"Okay, honey bunny! Let's make a list of everything missing and rank them in order of priority. We'll log them in your calendar so you know what to do every day! Stay on task! You can do it! We'll do it together! We got this!"

"That's it. I don't care. Pass or fail. This is up to you. I'm out. I'm not even looking at the student portal anymore."

"I see on the student portal that you haven't even started that alternative project. It replaces your lowest grade! Oh, I'll just do it myself. Move. I can't do ninth grade again."

"Fine. Repeat ninth grade. This is *your* project to do or don't do. I am a forty-six-year-old grown lady who already graduated from high school. I am not responsible for freshman geography. I don't need to know where all the countries in the world are."

"We can do this! Let's print out the spreadsheets and make a check-list! Let's set up a workstation at the dining room table so I can help you as you go! We are going to knock this out!"

"Just go back upstairs and pretend to work up there so I don't have to watch. Sure hope your teachers will accept Snapchat hours in place of assignments. I am not investing anymore. I will not say one more word about school."

"LAST DAY TO TURN IN MISSING ASSIGNMENTS! YOU CAN DO IT! JUST WRITE ANYTHING DOWN AND HIT SUBMIT! ANY WORDS AT ALL! JUST ANSWER C! PLEASE, GOD, WE'LL TAKE A D-! WE'LL TAKE STRAIGHT D'S! D'S GET DEGREES! GOD, IF YOU AREN'T LISTENING, THEN I'LL MAKE A DEAL WITH THE DEVIL! WHO WILL HELP US????"

And that is why I am locked in my bedroom with a bottle of cabernet sauvignon and a weighted blanket when my friends text me to pack some sunscreen. I don't know how I can be gone for five days, but I figure only one of us is making it out of COVID school, and I want it to be me.

The world is opening back up cautiously, so we mask up and fly on a half-empty plane to a resort in Cancún allowing 20 percent capacity. Everything is weird. Most of us haven't flown in almost a year. All public spaces contort around distance seating, distance sunbathing, distance drinking. We take COVID tests at check-in and are granted safe entry fifteen minutes later. We made it.

We walk straight through the hotel to the deck overlooking the ocean. The five of us stand there silently, staring at the waves, the warm breeze remarkable in January; other than Colorado, we have barely left our town in ten months. My sister Cortney slips her hand in mine. I reach for Jenny's hand. She reaches for Shonna's, who reaches for

Megan's. None of us say anything or move. We have been so sad and isolated and overwhelmed. The ocean feels like a miracle.

That evening, after laughing poolside with chocolate martinis for six hours (inadvisable), the girls call me to one of their rooms. I walk in to streamers, banners, posters, a veritable party pack-muled in from Austin. Gifts line the dresser. They give me cozy tie-dyed jammies, panties with weird cat graphics and dirty slogans like "Lick it before you stick it" and "All you can eat" (charming). Because I recently told them Jason Bateman was my perfect male type, I receive not only a mug but also a T-shirt with our faces photoshopped together and the caption "This is our happily ever after" tagged with "The Batemans" below. The back of the mug says "I love you more," which they explain as "You love him more because he has never heard of you."

We laugh until we fall on the ground. It is all so outrageous, such pitch-perfect best friend behavior. We have made it to a silly nonsense portion of the story. I think for the millionth time that these girls are among the greatest loves of my life. At the six-month mark, they have seen me through the worst of it. We cried every tear there was to cry. They helped me through my birthday, Thanksgiving, Christmas, my anniversary, New Year's; the first round of firsts after divorce is so disorienting. We raged, screamed, swore, brainstormed—whatever the moment called for. They didn't step wrong once.

Turns out, some love actually is forever.

Sensory Shift

I watched a video once where a blind man walked down the street making clicking sounds to gauge his surroundings. In the absence of sight, his hearing became hyperdeveloped. He grew proficient in echolocation, fine-tuning the frequency of his clicks and detecting objects and their distance by the returning sound wave. His heightened hearing became so accurate, he could draw a sketch of a room after clicking his way around it.

Marriage takes up a lot of real estate, as it should. That is your life partner, your home ally, your parenting comrade. You said "I do" and then you must. There is a lot of doing in marriage. Some of the equation is simply required—soccer games, yard work, the joint business of running a family—and some is important upkeep—date nights, vacations, alone time together. Your spouse is your number one, the largest slice of the pie chart.

Having lost the material dimensions of marriage, I find I have undergone a sensory shift; I am radically attuned to my girlfriends. Four of us live 0.02 miles apart: Megan and I on one street and Jenny and Shonna on another. We have matching Vespas and a golf cart should this distance prove too daunting, and I don't go one day a week without them.

We blare old country music all over our small town on the golf cart, skipping the songs I still can't listen to because they know "Better Man" by Little Big Town once made me pull my Bronco over on the side of I-35 and sob. We pile into each other's beds to watch movies and text the corresponding husband the next day apologizing for spilled wine on his side. We crowd in hip to hip on one couch while the other one is empty.

We go on "date nights" with the husbands and reserve a table for seven. I tell Tray and Jenny we have been friends longer than most marriages, so I am now married to them and we'll make retirement plans and figure out what to do with the misbehaving grandkids; they name our group chat "Thruple." We celebrate Steak Dinner Valentine's Day at their house—three couples plus Jen, and lest anyone think they feel sorry for me, Tray tells me to bring two sides because there is no free ride just because I got a dumb divorce.

I can no longer imagine any meaningful life without their constant presence, and at the risk of sounding too earnest, I am in love with them. In my marriage, I stopped seeing and being seen. But in its absence, I became highly tuned to the stunning symphony of friendship, which, it turns out, can guide you all the way back home.

Hanging Plants

Look, I'm not trying to make a big deal out of it, but six months later, I've kept the two hanging plants on the front porch alive and vibrant.

Six. Months.

That is my plant record by around five months and two weeks.

I didn't mean it to, but the repaired front porch accidentally became a metaphor and the plants a talisman. Sure, I have no precedence for functional plant care, but I have also never been a single mom. Sometimes we learn new things.

My plants and I, we are living.

We are living.

We are living.

Neither of us thought we'd make it, but here we are, living.

Mother's Day

My babies and I have been *through it* this year. We rallied around each other relentlessly. So why did I send a grabby, desperate, worried, fake-ha-ha text that Sunday was Mother's Day and they still had time not to forget?

"Mom. Chill. We already have this."

"Mom, you are two weeks behind."

"Mom, we already have a plan but thanks for making it weird."

God, motherhood is surprisingly fragile. I always assumed moms just knew everything and had no doubts or really even feelings. Turns out we are anxious, tender human people. Man, can we wobble. My neediness came out sideways and *bam* I acted passive-aggressive and controlling.

My kids give me flowers and chocolate strawberries. Remy wraps my favorite chips. They detail every inch of my car inside and out. They buy me a two-hour massage. They punch out my entire yard task list.

They rallied. Of course they did. First Mother's Day without a partner to spur them on, so they did it themselves. The kids and I have loved each other beautifully for ten months: one million family group texts, memes, dinners, late nights, sleepovers, porch time, trips, long calls, sushi, shenanigans. We've paid attention to each other.

What a fucking mess this rupture has been. God, I didn't want any of this for them. For our family. I did not want my kids in therapy over divorce. I'm sick to death over the broken relationship with their dad. I hate this loss for them.

But somehow love keeps mattering. It seems to be pulling through as the lead story. I guess it is true that love bears all things, believes all things, hopes all things, endures all things. What a miracle. What an absolute miracle.

Dr. Amadi

Ten months into this free fall, my life is in order. That is to say, my affairs are in order. My new file cabinet is color coded, labeled, and full to the brim: "Insurance," "Cars," "Divorce," "Will," "Mortgage" . . . everything has an organized folder. I have transformed from a girl who didn't know her bank password to one who checks all her accounts every morning before 8:00 a.m. I have overfunctioned so severely, it is a fever dream.

Turns out, adrenaline can last longer than it is supposed to. All that increased blood pressure enlivens the heart, lungs, muscles; it allows the body to respond to an emergency. How else can we outrun the killer?

In matters of the soul, the house is in trouble.

My chest is so, so tight, every day since last July. I've been telling my friends for months: "You guys, I *actually* have a broken heart. I'm serious. I can feel it. It feels broken."

Additionally, a child is suffering. This year has been too much. Grown adults buckle under less, for God's sake. The load-bearing walls are giving way, and we are in trouble. I am alone in this. I have no parenting partner. I am terrified and overwhelmed beyond explanation. I don't know how to break these cycles of darkness. We are losing our grip.

One month before the end of school, the crisis peaks. I onboard every intervention that exists. I email all teachers with the same message: "We will not be back at school this year, and no missing assignments are getting done. Please, please just pass us."

We are with doctors. At least for the next few days, my child is safe. Alone with the nurse, I try to answer her questions, but I am seeing black spots. My head is swimming. I am losing equilibrium. My broken heart is flaring, and I cover my chest with my hands.

"Ms. Hatmaker, lean back."

I am drifting. I feel a cuff go on my arm. She calls in a colleague. They are telling me to breathe deeply.

"Your blood pressure is 175/125. You are about to pass out. You can't drive. Who can we call to come get you and take you to the emergency room?"

My mom and sister pick me up thirty minutes later. It is a Sunday. Emergencies are no respecter of office hours. We start driving to an ER closer to my house. In the front seat of my mom's car while Cortney drives mine behind us, I have my first full panic attack. It is horrendous. I can't breathe and am so scared, I just sob. I feel like I am going to die and am afraid I actually might.

We make it to the ER. It is noisy, overstimulating, crowded. I am having a physical emergency, but I'm the only one who thinks so. A bored receptionist hands me paperwork. I can't do paperwork. I need someone to help me. We cram into the waiting room while I am drifting in and out of lucidity. Forty minutes later, still waiting, my sister says: "Your regular doctor's office has after-hours appointments available. Get in the fucking car." We are there ten minutes later.

We walk into my familiar clinic. It is absolutely quiet, absolutely empty. The lights are low. The music is soft. It is gentle and calm. The receptionist takes me straight back to the on-call doctor. I go from parking lot to patient room in under two minutes.

Dr. Amadi walks in. He is West African, as tender a grandfather with a medical degree as you could ever hope for. My face is streaked with tears. I haven't slept in two days. I am disheveled and scared and clearly unwell. He quietly takes my blood pressure, pats me kindly on the knee, and says: "Tell me everything."

I start minor: "I think my child and I might both die."

"Mm-hm." Pat, pat. "You're here. You're going to be okay. I'm here to help."

At this kindness, I begin sobbing. I spill everything: July 11, betrayal, financial chaos, divorce, single parenting, COVID school, depression, mental health crises, bone-chilling fear, exhaustion—and as I soak the front of my shirt, I am so disassociated, I look Dr. Amadi dead in the face and promise unironically: "I am actually really strong."

This dear man looks at the woman on the table with a BP of 175/125, face swollen from crying, who sweat through her clothes from a panic attack and couldn't even drive herself here, swearing she is not falling apart while she falls apart, and he says this:

"Jennifer, your body has done so much. It got you this far. It worked overtime on adrenaline for almost a year, and it is simply telling you it can't do any more. It has gone as far as it can on its own. That's all. It helped you survive. Now it is time to help your body back."

Something about this is so precious and tender and absent of shame, I feel the fight drain out of me. I surrender instantly. I yield to the obvious truth and lay down the last vestige of resistance. My best friend has carried me as far as she could. What a partner. What an absolute warrior. She fucking got us here. She gave every ounce she had toward our survival for 305 days. She labored and endured and worked and rallied and fought and held everyone else as long as she could, but bodies aren't meant to run on adrenaline that long, and she finally dropped from fatigue.

My child and I hit our breaking point on the same day, and literally the second I knew my kid was safe, my body collapsed. In two different places, we are surrounded by doctors determined to help us recover. Kind, gifted hands are comforting us, assessing us, caring for us. What outrageous fortune.

I decide to love my dear body.

We put her on blood pressure meds.

We put her on Zoloft.

We put her on antianxiety pills.

I give her nervous system and heart and adrenals and immune system and neurological pathways the first breath of fresh air in almost a year. I give her rest. I relieve her from the unsustainable burdens she has carried. I take her out of the arena and treat her like a good mother would.

Addendum: Dad

After three days of emergency rooms, rollaway beds, and facilities, I come home to a full house. My poor extended family is flattened. I am so physically and emotionally bankrupt, I can barely function. My dad is asking questions; I mostly just slump over. Someone puts me to bed.

I wake up to a long text from my dad:

> I had difficulty driving home after seeing you. My eyes were burning. My heart ached. Emotions are getting the better of me now. The worst feeling is to see one of your children struggling to the point it affects her well-being physically and mentally. When the next day doesn't get any better. Only seems to get worse. And as much as a parent has an overpowering desire to intervene with the answer and fix things, make all the hurt go away, we can't and carry a sense of failure and regret. The hard case of reality sets in and crushes that desire to make everything right again, like when you were a little girl and Dad could fix most of the disappointments. Not anymore.

> I cried going home. I'm close to bawling now. Grieving over how fragile you appeared to be. Wanting so desperately to make the sun shine again for you. Make the hurt, the desperation, the loneliness of single parenting and the pressures of earning a living all go away. There can't be anything more heart wrenching than not being able to make things right. The promise that just popped into my mind is that we are overcomers. Whatever is born of God overcomes the world. Our Heavenly Father is the real fixer. I was only the temporary stand in. We'll get through this.

As I consider how to get my own child through a crisis, my dad offers me a master class in parenting: I can't shield my kids from suffering nor fix it when it happens. The best I can do is see them, name their pain, grieve it with them, and promise to stay close. This is the very best we can do, the very best any kid could ever hope for, even if she is forty-six years old.

It's Complicated

I was a Church Baby from the womb. I came up through the youth group, church camp, See You at the Pole, purity culture, Acquire the Fire, DC Talk, rededicate your life to God subculture. I went to a Baptist college and got married at nineteen because sex and young adulthood only belonged to marriage.

I was a pastor's wife through several iterations of church: conservative formal church, cool church with designer jeans and bands, outward-facing missional church. My husband and I started our south Austin church from scratch in 2008. I've spoken and taught at every type of church, denomination, and conference.

I haven't attended my church in almost a year.

I simply don't know how to be in that sanctuary.

I started that church with a partner, so now I feel a strange disorientation, a founder whose life veered shockingly off course, alone with the ghosts of the sanctuary. I cannot bear the idea of everyone's pity or confusion or pain. They have every right to feel flabbergasted by our divorce, and I'm scared to absorb their feelings. We built this community as prototypes of church leadership, but our story is now calamitous. The Hatmakers?? Surely not them. Surely not like that.

From a wider lens culturally and politically, most of what I was taught as gospel standards turned out to be optional values abandoned for power, greed, or lies. The church that raised me bears almost no resemblance to the one dehumanizing refugees, defending white supremacy, and aligning with a morally bankrupt autocrat. To put it succinctly: Organized religion, once my happy place, truly confuses me. I am adrift inside it for the first time in my life.

I remain stubbornly attached to Jesus, devil be damned. Something inside that connection stays tender. My therapist told me: "You are now able to be known in new ways. You have never experienced God's love for you in these broken places, because they have never been broken before." So that is an unfamiliar side of God I am figuring out, the one who loves me decommissioned, the one who understands the sanctuary ghosts and lets me watch *CBS Sunday Morning* instead of church without shame.

Church right now feels like my best friends, my porch swing, my children and parents and siblings. It feels like meditation and all these leaves on my twelve pecan trees. It feels like Ben Rector on repeat. It feels like my kitchen, and my table, and my cozy reading nook. It feels like Jesus who never asked me to meet him anywhere but in my heart.

I guess God is near and good and dear wherever we are, however we are. Inside the sanctuary but also outside it too, because apparently the Spirit will be found by anyone looking. Wherever we meet the divine, and love, and healing, and beauty, it is good.

It is truly good.

This is all I know for now.

Question

For the first time ever, I am considering why so many people don't come to church when their lives unravel. This has never occurred to me. Church has been the bedrock of my life since I was a fetus. I have probably not missed a dozen Sundays in my entire life until March 2020. Why is my response relief and not grief that I just can't go?

Table

It is disorienting to lose a whole person from your ecosystem. One less chair, one less stocking, one less plate, one less cell number in the group chat. I am very used to seven; six feels small, paltry even.

Other areas shrink too: my social ability, my hosting appetite, my relational capacity. I have always lived expansively. I love a full table, a crowded porch, several lively group texts at once. Sure, come on over. Sure, bring anyone you want. "Mom, how do you maintain, like, five engaged friend groups?" Sydney always asked. "I struggle with one."

I am willing to accept some atmospheric changes—I have no choice after all—but I miss this part of me. I don't recognize this person ghosting the Voxer group, locking the front door, declaring text bankruptcy. Surely I don't have to abandon the tether to everyone who stayed?

My friend Jackie comes over without asking to power wash my sidewalks. She is like this. She once led a book launch parade down my street wearing a giant inflatable dinosaur costume. In the impending summer heat, she blasts the spring grime off the walkways inch by inch. Beautiful white stone reemerges. I see her staring out at my one-acre yard, the scene of countless parties, concerts, barbecues, Christmas Eve services, even a wedding. This has been the happiest gathering place, holy ground if you believe in that sort of thing.

A week later, we are sharing the hot honey pizza at Neighborhood's Kitchen on the Colorado River, and Jackie says:

"Jen, I had a vivid dream that you built a huge table in your backyard that could fit everyone you love. Like, huge huge. Way back in the clearing. You strung it with lights and gathered people around it like you always have. It was so clear."

Something about this vision reaches a beloved interior place that has become small, and it inflates on contact, like a balloon in a collapsed artery.

I begin to see it. Not just the table and benches, but the faces, the laughter, the stories, the memories waiting to be created. I can feel its life, like blowing on an ember that almost went out.

I turn to my bests, Jenny and Shonna, with their design know-how: "Can I hire you to project manage something for me? It is sort of over the top."

One month later, in the emptiest part of my yard, stone by stone, beam by beam, plank by plank, artisans and carpenters have built a twenty-eight-seat custom table on a gorgeous stone slab, each piece exactingly cut by hand. A long stone serving counter with storage runs parallel to the table. Lovely potted flowers flank each corner. The overarching pergola smells like freshly cut cedar. The whole patio is strung with twinkle lights and warm lanterns. It can fit five basketball teams.

It is the dream.

At twilight, my favorite time of day, I walk outside alone and run my hands over the custom-built table. I imagine the memories we will make here. One person gone does not beget an empty life. I think about the people I love and the guests I will invite and the holidays we will celebrate and the dinner parties I will host, the part of me I miss that shrunk this year. My people are still here. I am still here.

It is not too late to come home to myself. Even now, I can build the life I want, and if that starts physically with planks and stones, string lights and planters, then I am on my way. A boat is built on land before it sees the vastness of the ocean.

I look at my beautiful table, empty for now, and know instantly: I will fill you.

part three

THE
BEGINNING

A Soft, Sweet Summer

From Rachel Cargle's Instagram, June 30, 2021:

I've decided that this summer I am gifting myself a soft, sweet, succulent one.

I'm picnicking in the park, I'm exploring the book piles I have resting on my shelf, I'm going to pick strawberries in the fields upstate, I'm indulging in the warmth of a lover in the cool evening.

I'm writing handwritten letters to old friends, I'm taking midday naps in the sun puddles on my terrace, I'm waking up early and sipping coffee on the park bench, I'm packing light for trips to the vineyard and trips to sea.

I'm dancing in the moonlight on sands on other coasts, I'm eating big bowls of salads for lunch and ice cream for dinner. I'm going to revel in my bronzed skin, I'm going to say yes only to the things that thrill me and let no be a complete sentence where my heart finds necessary.

I'm going to make rest a verb and healing a decree. I will write in my journal while on sailboats and I will read rocking lightly in a hammock under a tree.

I don't know if gifting myself an entire season is an option but I've always let my curiosity prove the possibilities.

Me Camp

We have made it to summer. Releasing the pressure of COVID school alone is a relief I barely know how to describe. We are stabilized, my child and me. But God are we rattled.

I will do anything to disrupt the cycle of isolation. We can't be stuck in this house sucked down into social media spirals. This is the moment for something drastic, a complete sea change. I'm thinking wholesome. I'm thinking zero screens. I'm thinking old-fashioned summer reprieve, an emotional rescue through a physical adventure.

At the eleventh hour, I sign my kiddo up for summer camp the entire month of July in Maine, the purest state I can think of, not that I have ever been there. The teens forfeit their phones upon arrival and retrieve them on the last day. It is the quintessential summer experience: kayaking, crafts, musicals, cabins. The staff is tender toward campers bruised from the pandemic; we aren't alone.

Because recovery still feels precarious, in a blaze of spontaneous glory, I say: "Honey, how about this: I will come to Maine too. The whole time you are at camp. So if you need me for *any reason*, I can be there in two hours."

Problematically, I don't actually know any cities in Maine, where to stay, or what the hell I am talking about. Go to Maine? For a month? By myself? What am I even saying?? I am just making shit up.

But this emotional safety net feels important for my child's security, and I have three weeks to figure out how to put my money where my mouth went. "Internet, does anyone know anything about Maine? Like, a town for example?"

A dreamboat in my community writes: "We are almost finished renovating a three-story 1880 convent in Bar Harbor. Do you want to be our first renter?"

First, look up Bar Harbor on a map.

Second, text my financial planner and ask if I can even afford to do this. Nod when he says, "Jen, for God's sake, you don't have to ask to spend your own savings."

Third, book our flights.

And that is how my kid ended up at summer camp in interior Maine and I walked into a renovated convent in Bar Harbor.

I went from my parents' house to a dorm room to the marriage bed before I exited my sophomore year of college. I haven't had a solo adult experience a day in my life. I have, quite literally, always belonged to someone else. I've never known the sound of solitude. I've never been my own good company. I've never even been to a movie alone.

I make not a single plan except to fly here; I barely even look anything up. My only aim is to be near my kid, and everything after that is . . . a question mark?

Turns out, Bar Harbor is *enchanting*. I fall immediately in love. First of all, I am wearing a sweatshirt in July while the Texas hellscape is hot as Venus. Also, I can't deal with the charm. The little town, the little cafés, the little park, the little harbor. There is a tavern called the Thirsty Whale. Sherman's, the oldest bookstore in Maine, has painted section labels like "Tall Tales" instead of "Fiction." Sleepy shop dogs are in every store and bar. Garden beds are exploding with hydrangeas. It is a Hallmark movie on the Atlantic Ocean.

Unfortunately, I discover I cannot quit smiling. I must look deranged, but here we are. Not only I am unbothered to be traveling alone, but I am under its delicious spell. I don't have an ounce of self-consciousness. Something independent in me sparks to life. I am here on my own dime, my own time. This whole experience belongs to me. I instantly reclaim the "Alone" label; last year's indictment becomes this summer's exoneration.

I hastily write on socials:

I have exceeded my acceptable exuberance level. I am a Labrador retriever. I am touching everybody on their arms and flirting with every single old person. I've pet all the dogs. I laid in the grass by the ocean next to a stranger. I've chatted up the bartenders and waitstaff and librarians and ladies landscaping the YWCA. Today I ride my cruiser bicycle! What are we to do with this cuteness??

I've decided this is my Me Camp. I took myself to camp and I love it here. Friends and kids are coming up in pockets, but I have tons of hours in the sun and cool air to myself. It is quintessentially perfect here, and I am going to let it woo me.

I didn't plan anything at all, much less intend to brand it, but like that, Me Camp is born.

Less by book and more by touch, I establish a few Me Camp best practices:

My default setting is yes. Whatever comes my way, whatever invitation, whatever opportunity, whatever connection—unless I have an unimpeachable reason to decline, the answer is yes.

Which is how I end up taking a tour of Terry and Bernard's estate on the water, including a three-hour impromptu lunch with bottles of icy chardonnay, bruschetta, fresh lobster ravioli, and Bolognese Tagliolini. Which is how I end up at my neighbor's handmade kitchen table for champagne brunch. Which is how I find the Harbor House Flamingo Festival in Southwest Harbor and buy a navy and red hand-crocheted lobster sweater mostly meant for babies but with one in an adult size. Which is why when Megan and Lisa visit, we find a local library giveaway and fill three moving boxes with vintage books and mail them back to Texas. Which is why I eat every meal at the bar (seat for one!) and make friends with whoever is sitting next to me: David, Christina, Todd, Erin, Michael—they become my dinner companions, travel compatriots, story keepers.

I manage my own expectations with a simple loving rule: I'll do whatever I want that day. If I am feeling social, I will talk to everyone I meet, make friends at dinner, go to the "Picnic by the Ocean" gathering I saw on a flyer. If I want a quiet day curled up on my green velvet couch in the renovated chapel with a book and blanket and afternoon nap, so be it. I will "should" nothing. No "I should be seizing the day better" or "I should be doing something different" or "I should go out" or "I should stay in." Only whatever my little heart is in the mood for with no regrets.

I take field trips by just getting in the car and seeing where I end up. We ride scooters to the top of Cadillac Mountain in Acadia National Park because the internet said it is the highest point on the Eastern Seaboard and the first glimpse of the rising sun in America. I have a beautiful lunch with myself overlooking the harbor—buttery lobster roll, crunchy homemade chips, and cold sauvignon blanc—while I devour the end of my third book. I walk three blocks every crisp morning to get a double toasted everything bagel from Slice of Eden, and I take a twilight cruise on what can only be described as a pirate ship.

I feel utterly, completely awake and alive.

. . .

Terry and Bernard have been partners for forty years. Standing outside with Bernard clad in a vintage gardening apron and Indiana Jones hat in his stunning yard, I say: "You have lived an extraordinary life. What is your best advice?"

"Jen, keep your arms and eyes and heart open to whoever comes to you, wherever you are. You are meant to let people in."

Addendum: First Date

With my child tucked safely into camp, I land in a tiny airport in Bangor, Maine. I have an hour and fifteen minute drive to Bar Harbor and am standing in a short line for rental cars. We all have masks on, and by the looks of it, most of us have been traveling all day to get to the northeast corner of the country.

An attractive man (from the nose up) is next to me. We start making chitchat: "Oh I'm here for a month . . . Yes, by myself . . . I had a weird year . . . No, I don't know what I'll be doing . . . Yes, I know it is outrageous . . . "

He hands me his card and says: "I'd love to come to Bar Harbor and take you to dinner on your adventure. Here's my number."

Some relationship math: My last first date was on October 17, 1992, when I was eighteen years, two months, and ten days old (last first kiss: October 18, 1992). I was married for 26.53 years and have been single for 355 days. I turn forty-seven in one month and six days. Amount of time spent on modern dating, including apps, dates, or even thoughts: zero seconds.

• • •

I make it to Bar Harbor. I fall hard. It snares me in its charming sorcery and all of a sudden I am a person saying yes to almost everything. Whatever I thought this would be multiplies by a thousand, and on the fourth day there, I pull his card out and text: Hey, it's Jen from the illustrious Bangor Airport, driver of a rented Camry while you got the fun Jeep. I am claiming the dinner invite you offered.

I then proceed to absolutely panic.

I google: What are men right now. How are the men. Who is out there. How do you date a man. What do men in their 40s do. What are dates now. What are dating rules. What are you supposed to wear. What do they wear. Do I pay. Who pays. Are there code words.

I text my girlfriends: I am going on a date tonight. They, to put it mildly, lose their whole shit. Embedded in a long Me Camp update, I tell my social media community: "Oh, I also have a date. Everyone be cool . . . ," to which the internet says *we will not be cool, we will never be cool, you cannot make us be cool*. I settle on leather leggings and a cozy black sweater and red lipstick since I have already lost my entire mind.

In what can only be described as super cute, he drives two hours to pick me up and, upon seeing me clean, dressed up a bit, and without a mask, says: "You look gorgeous. I bought this whole outfit at L.L.Bean on the way here, including the shoes!"

The evening is, truly, as lovely as it could possibly be. We eat lobster, drink cold white wine, tell a million stories, laugh and joke. Everything feels easy. To my great surprise, I remember how to flirt, and it's pretty fun. Wrapped in his sweatshirt, we end the night sitting on a huge flat rock jutting into the harbor, kissing under the stars while my friend Megan stalks me from Texas on Find My Friends, convinced he drowned me in the ocean.

• • •

I text him late that night: Thank you for making me laugh and feel happy. You are the first date/first kiss guy in the story. There will only be one.

I lie in bed and smile at the ceiling for an hour.

Wow. Guess who's not dead.

Last first date (updated): July 5, 2021.

Relief

I pull into the parking lot to pick up my camp kid after one whole month of counselors, hiking, cabins, no phones. I fielded not a single panicked call begging for an early pickup, despite my worries.

I get out of my rental car, scan the crowd of camp teens, and spot a beloved face. It takes me three seconds of assessing body language to know instantly:

My kid is back. Thank God.

Camp saved us both.

Addendum: Four Years Later

Bar Harbor became an accidental template for the grandest gesture I've ever repeated: one month of summer solo travel, small northern town, near water, cool weather, walkable and bikeable, charming community, something that belongs in a Hallmark summer romance movie . . . but the romance is with myself.

July 2021: Bar Harbor, Maine

July 2022: Grand Marais, Minnesota

July 2023: Lambertville, New Jersey

July 2024: South Haven, Michigan

July 2025: TBD

July 2026: TBD

July 2027: TBD

July 2028: TBD

And on it shall go. Me Camp is the most outrageous, over-the-top, irrational thing I've ever done, and it changed my life.

Dream Again

I recently heard this sentence: "The trauma someone else created is not your fault, but dealing with it is your responsibility."

There comes a moment even with the most life-altering, painful loss, truly no matter how bad it is, where I eventually have to say:

I am a powerful co-creator in my own life.

The path of victimhood is readily available: endless rehashing, stalking, blaming, inertia, shame, paralysis, stagnation, fear. And to be honest, those have their place. We don't emerge from trauma immediately self-actualized. Some of those responses simply halt forward progress while our stunned hearts reckon with reality. There is a time to be fully and completely undone, because we are human.

But at some point, those responses are no longer "what someone else did that I am stuck with." I am making those choices and they are my responsibility. What I do with my pain belongs to me alone. (Note to Melody Beattie: *I can be taught.*)

So I am dreaming a little again. Me Camp gave me back something important. I am a powerful co-creator in my own life. I always have been. And my life is right now. I am not waiting on anyone or anything to "happen to me." I am not waiting on justice. I am not waiting on a relationship. I am not waiting on some future thing I'm only guessing at.

It is up to me to start filling my big table with people and laughter and delicious food and beautiful new memories. I want to gather family and friends under the stars and toast the Good Life, because the Good Life is right now. I've always had it. I didn't lose it.

I decide not to wait for an apology or affirmation or some nebulous future stage. I can't wait for better timing or better circumstances. I won't wait for anything that depends on someone else, because that is neutralizing my power. I'm done sleepwalking through my own story.

The Good Life is now, and I am its co-creator. So I will create it.

Frances

I am interviewing the inimitable Frances Mayes, author of *Under the Tuscan Sun*, on my podcast. She wrote her best-selling novel based on her personal experience. If you cornered me and my daughter Sydney and demanded our favorite movie, we would refuse to pick between our top two:

1. *Notting Hill*
2. *Under the Tuscan Sun*

Frances, in a word, fascinates. Who uproots a normal American life and sinks her entire worldly savings into a ramshackle Tuscan villa? You moved to Italy because . . . you just decided to? Her story is fantastical. It is theatrical. I am obsessed and envious and inspired.

This interview is centered on her latest book, a memoir about location, a sense of place, the various homes that make up our story. What places build us? What do we carry in our bones and memories, our palettes and senses? What does home mean, the one we were born into and the ones we later choose?

Frances, what is the most formative in-between home you ever lived in? A transitional home if you will.

The short time I spent in France was a huge transition period. At that time, I thought my husband liked to sail too much, my daughter was totally into horses, and I was just putting my family first, first, first, first, not even thinking about myself having any kind of particular future. Maybe I was going to write a few things when I had time or something.

But I went alone to France to a cooking school. It was actually with Simone Beck, Julia Child's partner for *Mastering the Art of French Cooking*. It was in Provence, similar to Tuscany in some ways, with eight other women, and we cooked every day. We had great times, we met chefs, we traveled around, but it was in a part of France where roses are gathered for perfume. You opened the door and could smell this air, and on long walks in the countryside, I got the feeling: *People get to live like this. Yes, I would like to live like this.*

I had not even taken a stance for myself as a writer yet. So at the end of that cooking school, I went back home and enrolled in graduate school. I was later asked to stay and teach in the department, and I started publishing. It was through those walks in the French countryside realizing that people do live like this, and I can too, that many years later I buy this Tuscan house in a similar landscape. I started that life where I'm cooking and having my friends over and writing books.

Who would have thought the change France engendered from where I was before? That little trip was a flip over for me. It was very subtle, but I look back and see where I made changes. You find these cross marks in the road where you could have gone either way. And I chose the life I wanted.

I could barely sleep that night.

People can choose to live like this.

What if Mary Oliver is right and this is our one wild and precious life? What if we really don't get any days back, and this whole life is ours to either grind our way through or throw our arms open for delight, for wonder, for joy and beauty and connection? What if we keep putting off happiness until later and later never comes? What if we hang doggedly on to "surely this thing will eventually get better" but it doesn't? Are we really just helpless recipients of stalled, drained, broken things, or do we have some agency? What if a life exists so full we would barely recognize it against our hustle and exhaustion and emptiness? Have we settled when we don't have to?

What if there is a different path, a different pace, a different peace?

Apparently people can choose the life they want.

Leap

From *Instructions for Traveling West* by Joy Sullivan:

Nothing my friends tell me shocks me anymore. No wild dream or unadvisable plan or moonshot idea. Recently, my friend told me she wants to move to Wyoming to be closer to horses. She tells me horses can hear your heartbeat from four feet away. That's enough for me right there.

Another friend is relocating to Peru. Another to Alaska in search of his true north. Another is adopting a child. Another is turning down a killer job so she can finish the book she's been trying to write for years. Another is leaving the man of her dreams for a woman.

Look, America is awful and the earth is too hot and the truth of the matter is we're all up against the clock. It makes everything simple and urgent: there's only time to turn toward what you truly love. There's only time to leap.

Feed These People

I had been married one year when I served my father-in-law canned ham. I was a culinary tragedy. A few years later, at age thirty on January 1, I decide on the spot to like cooking and figure it out instead of resenting kindergarteners for wanting to eat again. I buy my first cookbook, my first real knife, my first head of garlic, and start watching the Food Network. Those hosts—Rachael Ray, Ina Garten, Sandra Lee, Pat and Gina Neely—put me through Culinary Homeschool and I emerge knowing how to grate fresh ginger and make a perfect cast-iron steak.

Turns out, cooking becomes my favorite thing.

In the earlier days of social media, I start posting dishes in my helter-skelter, rambling, melodramatic way of "writing recipes" (a dereliction of definition) that are part cooking instruction, part stand-up comedy. It's all fun nonsense. I love it. My two favorite things on earth combine: food and writing. The stakes are zero because who cares about a random Facebook post about Duke's Mayo on a Tuesday?

Ridiculously, my online community is highly responsive to the funny food writing. Women are pinning my recipes before I even understand Pinterest. I field constant requests for a cookbook but "only if you write it exactly like this." In a move of hubris, my community starts an online petition to *force* me to write a cookbook. Thousands of women sign it. WTF.

My agent insists I read the room and very casually puts a proposal together for a weird, non–industry standard cookbook tentatively called *Feed These People*. We are polishing it up for submission when July 11, 2020, hits and life grinds to a halt. A couple of months later, my agent asks if it is time to send it out:

"Oh no. Everything is ruined. The center point of the whole project is feeding my family. It's all Hatmaker stories, and we're broken. Sorry about this failed project, and I guess this failed life."

"Jen, do you still have children?"

"Yes. There are so many of them."

"Do you still have siblings?"

"Yes. We are so loud."

"Do you still have brothers-in-law and sisters-in-law and nieces and nephews?"

"Yes. Marrying into our wild family is a real ordeal."

"Do you still have parents?"

"Yes. They survived us."

"Do you still have best friends?"

"Yes. They are my life."

"Then feed these people, girl. Get busy cooking."

And in the worst year of my life, a one-off cookbook project pulls me out of my head and drops me into the kitchen. In between therapy, doctor's appointments, and the ebb and flow of grief, I spend one trillion hours chopping, dicing, roasting, tasting. I feed my people with unhinged menus because test kitchen is weird, so they all get used to eating Braised Short Ribs with Blueberry Almond French Toast Bake and a side of queso.

As a writer this year, I can't form one coherent sentence about women's emotional health, but I can manage tacos. This project lets me be creative. It lets me be silly. It lets me be nurturing. It doesn't require leadership or focused advocacy or wife status, none of which I have. It puts laughter back in my life, my best people around the table, coconut shrimp with hot honey in my belly.

I tell my editor: "Even if no one ever reads this, every second was worth it. Because I loved it. And it loved me. This cookbook was my companion on the road back to myself, and I will always think of it like a best friend."

"Aw, that's sweet, Jen. We're going to go ahead and hope people buy it, thanks."

It's time to shoot the cover. The publisher wants the final shot in my kitchen, which makes pragmatic sense. Every cookbook on my shelf has a cover in a kitchen, no exceptions. That is where cooking is done. It is on-brand, as the kids say.

So we shoot two full days in my quirky 1908 kitchen. There I am holding the homemade pizza. There I am with a glass of wine. There I am at my oven. We send the proofs over and everyone is delighted. I am cookbook author in my kitchen where I cook food, and this makes sense for the general industry.

I lie awake not happy with it. It isn't right. Something isn't right. It's technically fine, but this project showed me that I am still a writer and still have a career and can still access my own little weird brand of magic. This cookbook said, "Chin up, dollface. You got this." Holding a pizza next to my sink doesn't honor the gravitas, like saying "Thank you" when someone says "I love you" for the first time. It is practically to print when I send an email:

"Team, can we reshoot the cover? I will pay the costs."

"Why? What don't you love? We are all happy with it."

"I need it to be somewhere else."

And in the middle of summer, I assemble my twenty-five best people on earth. The photography team returns to my home and styles the most gorgeous setting imaginable, and exactly at twilight, my favorite hour, with the twinkle lights on and the lanterns glowing and ten dishes beautifully plated family-style and my beloveds arranged and seated . . .

. . . we shoot the cover at my outdoor table.

I filled it.

Lonely

I am surprisingly awake.

For the most part, this feels electric, like I lost my keys but somehow started my engine with two live wires instead. All unexpected, yes. But neither am I still stranded on the side of the road. At some point you restart by hook or by crook and put your car back in drive.

But being alive again contains a low-register melancholy. I keep getting still to find the location, and it is vaguely tied to a sense of longing, of missing something, a feeling I don't have any precedent for, so I don't know what to do with it.

It is like an empty space where intimate love is supposed to belong, and I just got healthy enough to feel it. For a while, it was all trauma, terror, and shattered dreams. But after doing so much required recovery work, I can finally feel the less dramatic emotion of . . . loneliness. Yay! Horrible!

Because my therapist is now the narrator of my inside voice, I am wondering if I might consider this feeling a tiny victory. Something I was unable to feel earlier because chaos overwhelmed everything else. I generally feel fury first, because it is easier. Anger has such a high ROI. It is urgent and blazing and directed outward. I feel it toward someone, something, some pain *out there* laced with adrenaline. And there is a place for anger, to be sure. My anger sailed the ship for a bit in the absence of any other fuel.

But maybe this feeling is telling me I have recovered enough to be tender again, that my heart survived and can still feel, still *wants* to feel. It didn't kill me. None of this destroyed whatever is lovely and gentle and vulnerable in me. Perhaps loneliness is a green flag.

This is a small miracle. Permission to celebrate it. I'm alive.

Triggered

Men are far more likely to not just remarry after divorce but remarry quickly. The statistics are clear.

Two months after he moves out, my husband has a new girlfriend, and we receive endless texts from neighbors who see them dancing at Maverick's and eating at Mudbugs and whatever else is inside the three-square-mile radius of this small town. We haven't even filed for divorce yet. They get engaged the next year. We find out from a curated photo shoot set to music on Instagram.

My reaction is severe. I fire off a bruising text asking why random IG followers know he is remarrying before his family. I am in a tailspin.

This goes unresolved, but therapy trained me to stay curious when I respond this viscerally. Dr. Hillary McBride, author of *The Wisdom of Your Body*, taught me to access the message my body is sending, because my first reaction is usually all heat, all intensity, all one-note emotion—*enraged* or whatever—but she says to then ask my body:

"What do you need me to know?"

And just like that, my body becomes a professor and I pull up a chair to find out what she wants to teach me. She has given me a pounding heart, searing heat from chest to forehead, shaking hands. My body is communicating to me, and she is my most trustworthy advisor. She will illuminate the path of wisdom if I am brave enough to follow her. There is something important to learn right now, and her immediate physical response grabs my attention. I've ignored her at my own peril.

Physical triggers are a clue that something is unresolved emotionally. I always thought they were about the person triggering me; *my* body is overreacting because *that* person is an asshole. *They* made me hyperventilate. *They* made me sweat through my shirt. *They* made my ears ring. *They* made the backs of my hands prickle. If that person would behave, my body wouldn't have this mess.

But if that were the case, I would be triggered by all bad behavior. I would be emotionally inflamed 24/7. My body would be constantly dysregulated. But she's not. I handle plenty of volatile experiences with a measured response because I've worked through the dynamics already: I've had hard conversations, drawn boundaries, processed forgiveness; I've poured water on those wildfires. Cooled ashes are manageable. I handle them every day.

So if the fire is still raging, my body is saying: "Something to be done here, sis."

Back to *Codependent No More*. Melody Beattie explains: "A codependent person is one who has let another person's behavior affect him or her, and who is obsessed with controlling that person's behavior. [. . .] But, the heart of the definition and recovery lies not in the other person—no matter how much we believe it does. It lies in ourselves, in the ways we have let other people's behavior affect us."

As long as I am deeply letting his behavior affect me, if the urge remains to tell him how to do all this better, I am still codependent. So in the quiet, regulated freedom of my own curiosity, I ask myself:

"Why is this affecting me so much?"

God, we can be so kind to ourselves if we are willing to learn how. This tender question asked in the safety of my own body quiets the chaos and allows me to examine what still feels so bruised:

I am disregarded for another woman again. How this affects me and the kids doesn't matter. I am raising them alone and he is getting engaged in a fancy hotel with a fancy photographer, and it isn't fair. He gets a whole new life while I have to manage the one he left by myself. I wasn't even worth the courtesy of a text. I wasn't worth anything. I wasn't worth anything at all.

Woof. Apparently, I am harboring some intense resentment. And leftover pain from rejection. And the recurring wound of disregard. And maybe a deep fear about my own worth. My body isn't saying this is all *true*; she is saying this is how I still *feel*. She never lies.

The absolute worst is how all of this is my problem. Full stop. This is not his problem, and he won't be the solution. If my well-being is predicated on his behavior, I forfeit every scrap of agency. I cannot remain at the end of his rope. That is an optional life sentence, and I don't want it.

Codependency work suggests "loving detachment" and I don't know which word is harder. I don't feel loving and I am clearly not detached, but this is my path out. Detachment seems most achievable, so I start there with help from Melody Beattie, who says "there is no precise formula for detachment," and find a way that works for me:

1. "Learn to recognize when you're reacting, when you are allowing someone or something to yank your strings. Usually

when you start to feel anxious, afraid, indignant, outraged, rejected, sorry for yourself, ashamed, worried, or confused, something in your environment has snagged you."

Oh, I am snagged all right. I had to put on fresh deodorant. By the way, I'll feel SORRY FOR MYSELF IF I WANT TO.

2. "Make yourself comfortable. When you recognize that you're in the midst of a chaotic reaction, say or do as little as possible until you can restore your level of serenity and peace."

Some of my new tools are quantifiable and I follow them like a script: Phone down. No more responding right now. Walk outside and sit in the sun. Let those sensations roll through, peak, and recede. Feel them. Breathe deeply: eight seconds in, hold for four, eight seconds out, hold for four. Don't resist. Get calm and stay calm. I swear the pause-and-calm-down thing is 80 percent of it.

3. "Examine what happened. Feel whatever feeling you have. Nobody made you feel. Someone might have helped you feel a particular way, but you did your feeling all by yourself. Deal with it. Then, tell yourself the truth about what happened. How serious is the problem or issue? Are you taking someone's behavior too personally? Did someone push your insecurity or guilt buttons? Is it truly the end of the world, or is it merely sad and disappointing?"

Ah, I don't love this. Fine. Upon examination, this engagement does not mean I am unworthy, unlovable, and inconsequential. It actually has nothing to do with me no matter how much I catastrophize. This doesn't really affect my life. The lack of courtesy is merely disappointing with a smidge of sadness. I work to rightsize the whole situation.

4. "Figure out what you need to do to take care of yourself. Make your decisions based on reality, and make them from a peaceful state. You are not responsible for making other people 'see the light,' and you do not need to 'set them straight.' You are responsible for helping yourself see the light and for setting yourself straight."[1]

The truth is that my ex-husband started a completely different life, and that life has very little to do with me. I need to bury the fantasy that he owes (or should voluntarily offer) me any information about his new family. If that hurts his relationship with our kids, that isn't my responsibility.

I delete the scathing text I have in queue for him. Detach.

I disabuse myself of the notion that I am owed anything. Detach.

I accept that this isn't my business. Detach.

I take responsibility for my own triggered insecurity. Detach.

I admit that my resentment around solo parenting is a separate issue. Detach.

I remember that I am loved and that has nothing to do with him. Detach.

A few days later, I am discussing this unfun roller coaster in therapy and admit: "I managed the detachment part but struggled with the 'loving' part."

"Oh, Jen, detachment isn't about loving *him*. It is loving peace and freedom more than chaos and anxiety. Honey, *it is loving yourself*."

In Defense of Her

It feels important to be clear that his new girlfriend who became his new wife had nothing to do with the end of my marriage. He met her shortly after he moved out. Yes, we were still measuring our collapse in weeks, not even months, but that particular cart did not come before the horse.

As someone blamed online for the end of my marriage in the absence of clarity, I won't allow assumptions against another woman unfairly either.

She wandered into our wreckage after the storm, but she was not the storm.

Ending the War

If at the end of my marriage I had tried to predict what "recovery" would look like, I would have guessed learning to trust again, forgiveness, grasping independence, mostly stuff of mind and management.

I had no idea recovery would ignite a loving, intimate relationship with my own body.

This may shock you, but purity culture + the beauty industry + capitalism + evangelicalism + patriarchy produced a crop of women who hate their bodies. Untrustworthy, hysterical, too fat, too thin, too old, too emotional, too sexual, not sexual enough, dangerous, selfish, fragile, unfit to be self-governed.

Thus we have been at constant war with our bodies as prescribed.

The rage I feel watching leaders who *assured* us we were the problem now repeal our autonomy while giving men in power a free pass. Male pastors embroiled in sexual abuse? We'll handle this in-house; no need to alert the authorities for family business, she is probably lying anyway. Women who cross state lines for a medical abortion? Put her in jail. Men who grab women by the pussy without their consent? Put him in the White House.

It was all a sham.

I will tell you this: I am finished listening to what a single person in these subcultures tells me about my body. I don't want to hear what they think of sex, agency, reproductive rights, body image, sexual identity, any of it. It has turned out to be a self-serving, power-protecting, women-subjugating enterprise with an opt-out for men, and the whole rotten ship can sink.

Here, grab my hand, reader. Let's abandon that rotting ship and turn our faces to the sun. Wouldn't it feel good to end the war with our own bodies? We have the right to honor them, the responsibility even. As Dr. McBride teaches us, our bodies are not an "it" but a "she" and "her" because they are not simply the container; our bodies are *who we are*. She experiences desires and perceptions and trustworthy instincts, and these are to be heeded, not hated.

We are walking around in a homing device, a lie detector, a lookout on the highest point of the ship. When my brain interferes with its conditioned impulse to defend abusive systems, my body overrides her immediately. She knows. She tells me the truth. She always tells me the truth. She tried so hard to warn me long before. *Molly, you in danger, girl.*

Our life's work is to reject the message capitalistic, patriarchal systems have conspired to craft. They have a vested interest in keeping us at war with our bodies. If we hate how we look, they own us. If we hate what we want, they dominate us. If we hate what we crave, they control us. They get to master us with impunity when we despise ourselves; we do their dirty work and make it easy.

Our bodies are beautiful, truly. Gorgeous inside and out. They are deserving of the good lotions, the good sex, the good words. They should be heeded like the safest, smartest, truest, most knowing source of wisdom possible, because they are. We must stop saying the cruelest things on earth to her. We simply must. Some entire institution wants you to berate her and benefits when you do. She doesn't deserve that hatred. She isn't your enemy; she is your best friend.

Let the ship sink. It was never going to keep you afloat, darlings.

Phoenix

From Elizabeth Gilbert's Instagram, December 28, 2018:

I've lost the dark and particularly female talent for self-criticism, and for tearing myself down. It feels like sacrilege. My mouth can't force the hateful words. And I can't bear it anymore, to hear another woman demean, degrade, or diminish herself. It shocks my senses and hurts my heart. To witness a woman denying that she is beautiful is like watching someone set fire to an art museum. It's like watching an angel drink gasoline. It's like watching a Phoenix rip off its wings.

Moments I Felt Beautiful and Free

Dancing and singing and acting for our parents in an "original program" having practiced six hours in our grandparents' Colorado basement with my sisters and cousins.

Spending hours on the worn library floor with books piled around me deciding what to check out for the week and adding them to the stack the librarian pulled already because "I think you would love these."

Taking the field at shortstop in the first inning with such confidence because no one's dad practices more ground balls, pop flies, and accurate throws with them than mine.

Redecorating my room for my twelfth birthday, I choose a turquoise fitted sheet, orange flat sheet, sky-blue pillowcases, and a bright yellow comforter. I pick out a hot-pink phone with oversized buttons and tack up posters of Duran Duran. Immaculate.

Standing by my Grandma King in her dedicated pink bathroom on pink shag carpet while she puts Avon lotion on my face and Mary Kay gloss on my lips and tells me "Us girls can't have too many nice products."

Receiving notes in the margins of papers from my teachers that say "This is a really beautiful paragraph" or "I read your essay out loud to my husband."

The recurring feeling of lying in my cozy bed at night with my siblings in their bedrooms, my parents downstairs, and our family safe and secure. Being unafraid and loved.

None have anything to do with how I look, how well I behaved, or how I secured male attention. These memories are nestled inside being smart, loved, unselfconscious, creative, curious, and known.

Storyteller

I am the oldest of four. The top three of us are girls, and raising us is a whole situation. Getting four children ready for bed is a gauntlet. We have an ironclad ritual at bedtime: Mom wrangles the operations— baths, tangles, jammies. We fuss and whine and run the sink water without actually brushing our teeth because kids are weird and gross.

Once she scrubs off the day's grime and returns us from the scourge of filth, Dad tags in. We know the drill. All three girls pile temporarily into one bed, usually mine. We burrow into the covers and make a clearing in the middle like birds building a nest. When conditions are right, we holler in unison:

"DAD! WE'RE READY!"

He lumbers in and claims his space in the clearing while we meld into him from all sides, a mess of skinny legs and bony elbows and still damp hair. Lindsay threads two fingers through his hair and sucks her bottom lip, our dentist's worst nightmare and Dad's kryptonite for staying awake. We are a pile of little girl puppies.

"Which story do we want tonight, girls?"

We have dozens of options at our disposal, all memorized, all favorites. We can pull stories from Dad's real life:

"The Time Dad and Uncle Tom Hid Under the Beds Upstairs When Greta Weber Visited with Her Mother and Never Came

Out to Play with Her Even Though She Called Their Names for an Hour"

"The Time Dad and Uncle Tom Flew Their New Toy Airplanes in the House and Ruined Grandma's Ceiling and She Called Grandpa at Work and He Came Home and Spanked Their Butts"

"The Time Grandma's Cats Slept on Dad's and Uncle Tom's Freshly Washed Cars and They Shot Them with BB Guns and Lied About It"

Or we can choose from Dad's colorful and also demented versions of the classics:

"The Little Pigs Last Stand: The Electrocution of the Big Bad Wolf"

"Granny's Revenge: How Little Red Riding Hood's Grandmother Double-Crossed the Wolf with Poisoned Bread"

"Goldilocks's Hostile Takeover of Little Bear's Bedroom"

We cue up Dad for our story of choice, then the tale begins. Heaven help him if he changes any details, because we correct him with swift rebuke ("No, Dad, you hid Grandpa's cigarettes in the bread bin, not the pantry"). His plot points are impeccable. The characters are legendary. The drama is extreme. His voice fluctuates getting lower and quieter and slower until THEN GRANNY CHOPPED HIS TAIL OFF WITH A MACHETE! I'm not saying it is nurturing so much as entertaining.

We scream and laugh and squirm with anticipation as if we haven't heard the story hundreds of times. Most nights, Mom has to extract Dad hours later, asleep among his pile of girl puppies.

Time magazine is interviewing me in NYC. I'm a writer and my books are selling, and it is important to establish credentials for authors. Literature needs some gatekeeping, for God's sake.

"Jen, do you have an MFA?"

"Oh, no."

"Undergrad in lit?"

"Nope."

"Communications?"

"Elementary education."

"Hmm, interesting. How did you learn to become a storyteller?"

I don't have the answer they prefer but one that is true:

"Bedtime."

Attachment

Some shared therapy: I am learning to reverse unhealthy attachment patterns. I have "avoidant" tendencies because I am conflict averse and aggression immobilizes me. In my marriage, that manifested as silence, withdrawing, and ignoring anything hurting or bothering me, plus ignoring my own behaviors too (bonus!). I shut those off and felt like I was being "easy." Of course, nothing could be further from the truth because withdrawal doesn't feel easy to your partner, it just feels disengaged.

Because I spent a year of therapy focused on my own patterns (therapists are *the worst*), I am learning new ways of relationship-ing, which includes transparent conversations, saying when something feels bad, listening without defensiveness, and conflict resolution prioritizing connection. Here is how it feels in my body:

Like I am being difficult.

Because I believed "silence = I'm easy" and "hard = bad," anything else makes me feel high-maintenance, my least-favorite trait. But turns out, grown-up conversations around feelings aren't high-maintenance, they are just maintenance, which relationships require.

These new practices feel terrible at first, but I'm not sure they are. When I've never had boundaries, then first employ them, I feel mean. When I've rarely listened to understand instead of just defend, I feel unprotected. Honesty feels dangerous. Forgiveness feels foolish.

Disagreement feels destructive. Explaining my needs feels selfish. Saying I'm sorry feels too vulnerable.

I just don't have muscle memory for healthy patterns, so they feel weird. I am used to dysfunction, which I defined as "normal." I set the wrong bar.

I suspect this can be overcome. When I know a practice is healthy, I am trusting it instead of my early feelings about using it. My therapist says those feelings of discomfort will recede, and I'll get healthy, connected relationships where both people matter and listen and solve things and love one another without creating a breeding ground for resentment, hyperbole, or disintegration.

Apparently everything gets to be all on the table. If I can get past my conditioning to be "easy," I think this might change my life.

Sex

I haven't had sex in a year.

Near the end of my marriage, there was a daily sexual mania when I thought we were working to reconnect. But before then, we'd stopped having sex for two years. To be clear, *I* hadn't had sex for two years.

I am so poorly trained to think about sex in any sane, healthy way, I am a ship without a rudder here. Purity culture pathologizes sex so thoroughly, I am conditioned to feel a small handful of emotions: fear, shame, self-disgust, aversion. Supposedly sex is reserved for marriage, but I'll be damned if I am walking an aisle before I feel a man's hands on my body again.

My friends, married for a zillion years, are all over the place as advisors. They've been having sex with the same partner since we permed our hair, and most of them grew up sexually shamed too, so what do they know? They range from "I would only have casual partners and hot escapades" to "I wouldn't have sex again until I die." I love them, but they are not a single sexual think tank.

Let's be fair: What do I know either? I had exactly two sexual partners in my life, and dear reader, I suggest we barely count anything in high school. Sex? Sure. A sophisticated sexual experience? Geez. What a free-for-all. Every man for himself!

An insidious fantasy of purity culture is that under the thumb of shame and fear, women will suppress all sexual impulses, then miraculously become vixens on their wedding nights. Legions of women have followed this script and found they are sexually paralyzed, unable to have sex at first. By design, the system snuffs out a natural sense of curiosity, experimentation, and unselfconsciousness.

When you are taught that sex and desire is bad, that *you* are bad for your own natural sexuality, well, you believe it.

I am trying to imagine how this sounds to a reader who was raised with a transparent, nonjudgmental ethos, and it must seem maniacal. But we were both overtaught and undertaught: total emphasis on abstinence with virtually no actual sexual education. Don't be slutty and have sex! But once you do, be awesome at it! And what slim practical instructions existed focused on male pleasure and unhindered female availability. Give it up to the husbands anytime they want it, ladies. They work so hard.

But I'm not a teenager trying to appease my sex-averse God anymore. I am a grown woman embracing all the ways I experience hunger. Women aren't supposed to want too much, but I always have. I have big dreams and big feelings and big vision and big appetites. I've always been too large for the prescribed container. And as I consider what a sexual renaissance might look like, I hear a ferocious roaring in my ears and it sounds like . . .

. . . desire.

Bumble

Heeding cues from my body and not just my overthinking mind, I think I am ready to . . . date? She has given me the internal prompts: from emotional self-protection, to dazzling independence, to a little heat, even to loneliness. Oh, sure, my brain has plenty of shit to say about this, because she is a Nervous Nelly, but my body is like: "Knock, knock, please find a way to get near a man."

My brain and body strike a compromise and decide to quietly make an online profile. Here is the extent of my knowledge on dating apps: Chrissy Metz said something on Instagram once about Bumble where "the women are in charge of choosing." This is the full scope of my intel.

I drink two glasses of wine at 11:30 p.m. and download the app. I'm not concerned about my profile because "the women choose on Bumble," so no one can even see me. I will peek in the window of men (?) and see what's out there. No harm, no foul. No big deal. No problem. No whoop.

I do the bare minimum to make a profile since it will be incognito. Required: three pics (the first three I find), my age, and location. I fill in zero of the other fields: kids, hobbies, job, whatever it all is. My profile looks like a bot: "Jen, 47, Buda, Texas . . . no additional information." Am I doing this right?

Anyway, I upload the pics and go straight to bed, having exhausted my gumption. I wake up the next morning and look blearily at my phone. The whole screen is full of notifications. I am trying to figure out if a group chat has gone off the rails when I notice the little yellow bee thing on every one of them.

Fun fact: Men *can* see you on Bumble, and apparently you do not need a single qualifying detail on your profile for 144 of them to Bumble you. Also, a bunch of them Super Bumbled me or whatever the hell it is called, and this is the reason God invented anxiety meds.

I have no idea what to do, so I start scrolling through them, and I am just saying it is a dark twenty minutes. I guess I didn't require any parameters either (I'm new here), so every man in a fifty-mile radius has Bumbled me, including the divorcés who are like "Excited to start another family with the right lady!" and I immediately die inside and become a ghost. The only way I am starting a family with some fifty-year-old man is if he adopts me and I become his daughter.

My brain steps in like a bossy bitch and says, "Just send a message to one and see what happens."

I have [checks notes] never texted a stranger with romantic goals. I pick one that doesn't look terrifying, summon any dormant game living in my body, and write:

Hi there.

God in heaven, deliver me from this mortal earth!! That is the best I could do. I even put a period at the end like a robot. Not ten seconds later:

Hi! How are you?

How am I? Well, I don't even know. I am texting a stranger I have zero information on at seven thirty in the morning and is this what dating is now because I am way too precious for this. Maybe my parents can arrange a marriage and I'll just show up to my wedding. Like the world's worst improviser, I give the exact opposite of "yes and . . . " and text back:Fine, thanks. (Comma and period included.)

Disastrous. It's like I've forgotten how to be a person. I turn off notifications, put my profile on actual incognito mode, and close my phone immediately. I cannot be trusted here.

Four hours later, I meet my best friends for lunch. Jenny, Shonna, Megan, and I are doing our usual everyone-talks-at-once-but-we-miss-nothing cacophony, and a rare gap opens. Very calmly, *breezily*, I mention I made a Bumble profile and things happened. The girls *scream*. One of them stands straight up and knocks her chair back. Someone grabs my phone and starts manically scrolling. They demand to see every word I texted, and all three are spouting loud shit at the same time.

I quietly pull my shirt over my face, burst out crying, and delete Bumble.

And that is the story of how I spent twelve hours on a dating app.

Forgiveness

The path to healing is circuitous and difficult to discern. Because loss can reach from behind and grab me by the neck on an unsuspecting Thursday afternoon, it is challenging to chart the mending.

But one sign is the slow progress from anger to something closer to forgiveness. The fire is extinguishing. It is stunning that an entire life can ignite and eventually become cooled to the touch. How could that ever be? What an impossible evolution.

And yet I find myself able to access, if you can even imagine this, compassion. Time has given me the capacity to see that two college kids, not just one, were handed a story and tried to play the roles. The grown-up versions of us became less and less compatible. Some super-young couples evolve along the same fault lines and some don't. Fundamental differences that seemed positively inconsequential when we were young became consequential, and the gulf grew gradually for the next two decades.

Having worked through my own trauma, I am able to better understand the trauma that severed him from himself. It doesn't excuse his choices but helps soften the blunt force.

It feels important to include that he is sorry. This matters. There are permanent consequences he will never outrun, but denial won't be one of them. It doesn't fix it, change it, or excuse it, but apologizing is not nothing.

"I'm so sorry, Jen."

"I forgive you."

It is simple, and that is all it can be, because the complexities are endless and ongoing. There is no tidy ending to twenty-six years and a shared family. We will navigate graduations, weddings, grandbabies. We have a long, complicated road ahead, but we can smooth it significantly with forgiveness.

Forgiveness is not foolishness. Foolishness would include no boundaries, no responsibility, no honesty. Foolishness would bypass accountability for pretending. A fool would diminish the consequences to protect the offender's conscience. Foolishness would open a door that should remain firmly shut.

But forgiveness sets me free. I hope it hands him some freedom too, but that is his to alchemize. Rupture and repair may be the highest expression of humanity, and it is its own reward. Getting there means there is some combination of honesty, humility, vulnerability, compassion; these are high-water marks. This *could* be one-sided work if the only option was to forgive without any meaningful contrition, but it would be harder. It can be done because I have agency over my own emotional condition, but it would certainly, certainly be harder.

But he closes the gap, and I am grateful he helps shrink the long road of healing. For both of us. His actions detonated the bomb, but he was not spared the carnage. Our joint disintegration only prolongs the recovery process for the entire family. It is a wondrous good for us each to heal. Our congeniality is a welcome contagion in what will forever be our shared ecosystem. I want my kids' dad to be healthy. I want his new life to be stable. I want the best version of him in our lives.

It is tenuous at best, but I slowly reach for goodwill.

Hope

I hope you're spending Christmas with your family
I hope you're writing songs that you love
I hope you're feeling happier than you've ever been
And I hope I never leave me again.

-Kelsea Ballerini, "Leave Me Again"

Untidy

Something I wish was a bit tidier this late in the book:

What is my deal with church?

Allow me to break the fourth wall and speak four years from where you are in this story: I'm still not going to church. The COVID explanation is long in the rear-view mirror, I'm afraid. I am conflicted at best and swing between relief and guilt.

My dad went to seminary when I was three and served on church staffs my entire life. I married a ministry major and became a pastor's wife before I was out of college. I have, frankly, seen too much. Church has been the scene of endless crimes. We have harmed and been harmed.

Sorting out my own church-related dysfunctions led to some difficult conclusions: My spiritual environment worked exactly as designed. I didn't mistakenly interpret the systems. I didn't hear it all wrong. The men-first hierarchy delivered as advertised. Organizing God is so vulnerable to human corruption, it should be the most terrifying venture on earth to attempt. No one means for it to, but add power, money, and arbitrary rules of engagement to any pure thing, and attrition is inevitable.

The few times I went back to the sanctuary, I spent the whole time fending off death by a thousand cuts: *That lyric isn't even true, that language doesn't work, that idea isn't that simple, that song doesn't even make sense.* Emotionalism played too heavy and honesty too light, the formal version of my desperate teen journals to God: "Nothing matters but You!" except things do matter to us and this song does not feel true. I am playing the role of Worship-Song Singer, choreography encouraged.

I found myself desperate for someone to say the grittiest, hardest thing. I wanted to hear the truth about being a human and trying to figure out life, and loss, and God. I needed the opposite of polished and produced. My friends in recovery suggest the church I am looking for is in any given dingy basement at an AA meeting.

Church meant everything to me for four decades, and I understand why it still does for others. Millions of churches are beacons in their communities. I was a lifer, so I've seen many a heart nurtured. I also see the small, simple congregations with a bivocational pastor in pleated khakis who loves his little flock and has never heard of modern PowerPoint. It is not all a bloated rock-and-fashion show with an abusive culture behind the curtain. I know this.

I genuinely honor *any* effort to know God, however mysterious an endeavor that is. Which is one reason I couldn't go back on Sunday mornings. Sitting there in my triggered cynicism felt like poisoning the room. Let this space be pure for those who find the Spirit in this way. If someone's church was on a hiking trail, I wouldn't scramble beside them disparaging all the poison ivy. God said "Come to me" and didn't add a caveat about where that is, so I don't get to either.

I currently find myself unable to attend church and unable to reject it, and I worry about this unresolved leadership, and then I remember, dear reader, that I am not your leader; I am your sister, and this is not a handbook. You are a grown-up and make your own choices. You get to look for the Spirit however you want, and you will find her. I bless the search for divine love, a journey with a million routes.

That leaves me in charge of me only, like Jesus and my mom and Melody Beattie have been trying to tell me. Worry about yourself and all that.

I am still finding God. Just not where I used to think he lived.

A Little Tidier

I can speak a bit more securely on this:

What is my deal with Jesus?

Outside the structures, I've discovered Jesus is way less fragile than I was told. He isn't rattled by geography or denominations or the f-word. He's not easily bruised. He doesn't scare. He isn't American or Baptist or Catholic or Republican. He's not mad or mean.

Dr. Dallas Willard, beloved biblical scholar and professor, answered the question "If you could describe Jesus with only one word, what would it be?" with this:

"Relaxed."

Stunning. The Jesus I grew up with was zero percent relaxed, but the Jesus I know now carries an ease I've wished for my whole life. It's hard to explain this new knowing except it lives in my bones and breath. Having lost the institutions I thought he favored, I've been shocked to experience his identical affection outside of marriage and outside of church.

This is a far cry from the deal I brokered most of my life where I secured spiritual approval by working my ass off. Look at me! Working! Leading! Teaching! Organizing! Serving! Giving! Behaving! I'm doing it, Jesus. Love me. Be pleased with me. See how hard I'm trying. Tell me it is enough.

Then I lost all my gold stars and learned I was enough the day I was born.

Jesus loves us, and we're all in.

The two of us now, we're relaxed.

Questions I Am Done Asking

Will this bother someone?
Am I asking too much?
Does he/she/they like me?
What is wrong with my body?
Can I handle this?
Should I just be okay with this?
Is it too scary to change this?
Is this making everyone else happy?
Are my needs an imposition?
Am I smart enough?
Am I brave enough?
Am I maintaining my lovability?
Is God disappointed in me?
Is being alone worse than being unhappy?
Should I keep hiding?

Questions I Will Ask Myself Forever

What do I want?
What do I love?
What do I need?
What does my body know?
Why not me?
What am I excited about?
Am I free?
Who does God say I am?
What do I care about?
How do I want to live?
How can I love beautifully?
Am I being honest?
Am I being true?
Am I happy with me?

A Love Note to Zoloft

Man, you did your job. You helped stabilize my wild, frenetic brain so I could get through the days, the months. You quieted the noise and gave me back the power to think straight. You calmed the raging fear and allowed me to remember that hope was coming. You stabilized the ship in tumultuous waters so I could steer it back to safety.

I did not want to take you because I have some garbage ideas about self-sufficiency, which my therapist laid waste to pretty quickly. I was fifty feet underwater refusing the life preserver. Then my gentle doctor touched me on the shoulder and said, "You have experienced great trauma and your body has gone as far as it can. Help your body help you."

I noticed around August my spirit was back. Couldn't remember the last tear. Felt the hope I inherited from my dad again. My dark night of the soul was mostly over. It was a hell of a year. But I climbed my way back to the sun.

So I carefully stepped down my antidepressant until one day, I quietly took my last.

For some of us, antidepressants are a permanent way to keep the ship stable, and thank god for them. They are not a crutch or escape hatch. As Dr. Amadi said, they don't indicate weakness. They are an invaluable partner to a steady, durable life. Renew them to infinity. Help your body help you.

For others of us, we need them situationally. We may not typically suffer from depression or anxiety, but life handed us pain our bodies can't keep up with. Meds step in like a crisis counselor and hold our hands until we get through. This was me.

Sending love to my sisters with the prescriptions, be they long-term or short-term. Well done. You are taking the best possible care of yourselves, and I am proud of you. There is zero shame in this, unless we should be ashamed of creating strong, steady lives for ourselves and the people we love.

Either way, thank you Zoloft. And Lexapro. And Wellbutrin. And all of you. Thank you for giving us our lives back.

The Most Me

I talk on my porch for three hours with dear friend Amy, smudger of my home. The next morning, she sends the following text:

I'm still so happy about your recovery and thriving. You are more you than you've ever been. A person I love has overcome and it's the best thing I've ever seen. You didn't once transition into your professional voice—that shift you've always done to protect and deflect. The wave of your hand, wry synopsis of your life, "enough about me" little wall you would erect at any moment. You didn't have to use it because you've dug in, done the hard work, and reemerged. I'm so proud of you.

I can barely read it through the tears.

I text back: Oh my god. Thank you. Thank you for bearing witness.

The thing is, I am. It's true. I have never felt more like Jen in my life. Everything I say and do, the way I spend my time and energy, who I love and how . . . I am *in* my life like I was always meant to be, wide awake.

Dear one, keep doing the work. Whatever that means for you: recovery, healing, trauma work, self-honesty, relational repair, full ownership, sobriety, grief, necessary endings. Do it. Keep slogging. Keep moving forward by the half inch. Hang on to the promise of your whole full life and get there.

We cannot fast forward or short-circuit this. It all must be felt, admitted, faced, owned, examined, allowed. All of it. There is no other way. It will seem impossible, then too slow, then just hard . . .

. . . and then you make it.

There you are. The most you you have ever been. Worth every tear, every therapy appointment, every hour you spent getting here. You invested in you, and you emerge. What a miracle.

Keep going, darlings. Wherever you are—in some ending, in the slow messy middle, starting to see the sun rise. You are worth this work. Your life is worth it. Go get it.

Close the Bones

I am with my longtime girlfriend Laura having dinner for my birthday. She is my best brunch partner and one of my two favorite woo-woo earth girls. Deep talk and good food are our specialties.

Laura is discussing her latest "healing retreat," which historically has included experiences highly nerve-racking to even hear about, but Laura is an open book to the universe and all her magic. She starts describing the closing ritual for every woman:

"There is an ancient practice from South American and Mayan cultures in the first forty days after giving birth called Closing the Bones. Women wrap large cloth shawls called rebozos around the new mother's legs and waist. On either side of her, they pull the shawls tight and rock her gently to guide her bones back into place and realign her muscles and tendons. They bless the new life she birthed.

"But it is highly spiritual too. It brings closure to the birth journey and returns the mother to her body. Closing the Bones signals a new beginning of strength. It is deeply tender and pulls the mother out of fight-or-flight mode and into recovery."

I am listening with great interest in how this ceremony applied since Laura's last birth (home, natural, midwife of course) was fifteen years ago. This wasn't a postpartum retreat, and some women there weren't mothers.

"Our guide explained that Closing the Bones is not exclusively for birthing mothers or even just women. It is for anyone broken open after a life-altering experience: divorce, loss, death, menopause, empty nesting. Closing the Bones releases the pain and signals that fight-or-flight is over. It is a ritual for anyone ready to come home to their body, back to their beloved self."

I feel a low hum in the back of my brain. I quietly reach for my phone and text "closing the bones" to myself under the table, because my body tells me when to pay attention. Something here is important.

Six weeks later, I walk nervously into a small, beautiful space greeted by Mexican traditional medicine practitioner Irasema. The cozy room is part science class, part ancient healing tools. Illustrations of the endocrine system, digestive system, muscular system line the walls while the fireplace hearth is covered in objects honoring her Abuela Juana and Tía Ma Ester, the elders who raised her in a healing sobador community.

I explain why I am here. How embodiment connected me to my own grief and ultimately my healing. That I am seeking closure in my soul through my body.

"Rebozo healing has been used by Mexican matriarchs to care for their families for centuries," she tells me. "It is less about closure and more about transitions. Very few experiences just end. They *change*. Your marriage may be over, but so much remains. Your family has just changed. You have changed. You can honor everything those years gave you. This is not a blunt ending. It is a grateful transition."

This is resonant. There will never be a version of me in which twenty-six years of marriage is a nonfactor. You don't put a lid on nearly three decades of life and store it in the attic. There is no me today without nineteen-year-old us walking an aisle, twenty-three-year-old us becoming parents, thirty-seven-year-old us adopting our youngest two, forty-two-year-old us starting to launch our kids. We built this family, and it still hums with life.

What I *am* releasing is the trauma, the anger, the suffering. It's my choice to hang on or let go. Those responses had their place, but none of it serves me anymore. I am moving into the next phase of life changed, and though I never imagined it possible at the bottom of the ocean, that changed me is better.

I take this resolve into the session, which begins with sobada, a Mexican therapeutic massage that can only be described as gently diagnostic. Every motion is specialized and located. Irasema's hands find the tightness, the scar tissue, the locked muscles between my ribs. She tells me when to breathe deeply as her fingers press out the pain.

As she works, I let my mind tell me the story of my marriage. I track it from its earnest beginning up through the early family years. I watch us growing up alongside our children. I see his work grow and my career begin, and I remember those building years with great tenderness. I catch flashes of memories: our first plane ride together, hospital rooms with new tiny blond babies, the sidelines of too many soccer and football fields to count, throwing surprise parties for each other, traveling the world, building our little church together, watching our babies walk across graduation stages.

In most ways that matter, it was a good story. I thank God for all it gave me.

As I lie on my back, Irasema unfolds the five rebozo shawls I'd been lying on to hang down on either side of the table. She pulls the right side of the blankets up and across my body, and from my left side, she uses them to rock my body gently. She repeats the wrap and rocking on the opposite side, a physical preparation for transition, shaking off the tension she'd just released with her healing hands.

Then starting at my feet, she wraps my body tightly with both sides of the rebozo, tucking the shawl under my legs. She moves up to each blanket until my entire body is wrapped as tightly as any human could manage. She begins singing over me in Spanish.

And I panic.

As if my body understands the ritual, I instantly feel the comprehensive weight of all the shock, all the humiliation, all the sorrow. My body gathers the pain remnants into one place, like dragging a magnet through spilled nails and watching them all merge. My heart starts pounding. My breathing becomes labored. I sweat through the blankets. I try moving my arms but they are bound too tight. Fear surges through me from head to toe. I am freaking out. I feel like a body wrapped for burial.

Just as I am about to tear the rebozos off somehow, Irasema stops singing and says quietly:

"Jen, you are safe in your body."

I get very still.

My body overrides my fear, and she breathes deeply, calming my nervous system, understanding her own power. I follow her lead. I let the rebozos finish their work as a burial shroud and trust my body to respond as she needs to. With tears, I bless the story of my marriage, and I bury the grief of its destruction. I bury the trauma. I bury the anger. I bury the fear of it all. I bury the story I expected and lay it in its final resting place.

Irasema somehow knows, and she takes a soft, small broom and begins sweeping my body:

"Release everything that no longer serves you. Let it drop to the ground where it will become compost for growth."

As she sings over me, brushing off the emotional debris, the burial shroud slowly becomes swaddling. I transition from panic to comfort. I'm not trapped in death; I am wrapped and held and loved and safe. I return to myself in full control of my breath, my heartbeat. The rebozos no longer feel restrictive but reassuring. My trustworthy body floods my system with serotonin, and every muscle relaxes. I cool down ten degrees. I have the strangest urge to sing. Fight or flight is finished. The funeral is over. I've made it.

Safe in my body, I gently transition to the rest of my life.

I close the bones.

Young Me

One recurring feeling is, surprisingly, a sense of compassion for the young versions of me.

Who among us can't look backward and realize how far we've come or how much we've learned or how deeply we've changed? This is how growth works, and there is no fast-forward button; it is a function of time.

It is tempting to disparage the earlier versions of myself, berate her for not knowing or doing better, but I prefer to be gentle with her instead. She was doing the best she could with what she knew. She got me to where I am today, and that counts for something. She ran her leg of the race. I am proud of her for trying her best and going as far as she was able. She was handed some harmful narratives that take most of us a lifetime to dismantle, so good on her for surviving those.

Directing so much love to the young versions of us today, dear ones. Proud of them for getting us here. Let us be tender with our earlier selves, like wiser older sisters, like nurturing aunts, like good, good mothers.

Flowers

i hope
when you come home to yourself
there are flowers lining the front porch
that were left from all the women
you were before

-Maia, *When the Waves Come*

One Last Poem I Love

"Rain, New Year's Eve"

The rain is a broken piano,
playing the same note over and over.
My five-year-old said that.
Already she knows loving the world
means loving the wobbles
you can't shim, the creaks you can't
oil silent—the jerry-rigged parts,
MacGyvered with twine and chewing gum.
Let me love the cold rain's plinking.
Let me love the world the way I love
my young son, not only when
he cups my face in his sticky hands,
but when, roughhousing,
he accidentally splits my lip.
Let me love the world like a mother.
Let me be tender when it lets me down.
Let me listen to the rain's one note
and hear a beginner's song.

-Maggie Smith, Good Bones

A Beginner's Song

"Well, I'll tell you this: Once I do start dating, I am for *sure* not falling in love with the first man I meet." -A thing I said.

Coming up on the holidays, I am in New York with my publicist Heather. That one-off cookbook project became a *New York Times* bestseller and we have a bunch of press and whatnot. When I look at pictures and clips, I can see that I am happy down to my bones. Joy has reached my eyes again.

We finish our appearances and Heather says: "Do you want to share a cab back to the airport?"

"Actually, I think I might stay one more night. I'm already here and I kind of want to see a show. Jennifer Nettles is playing the lead in *Waitress*, and I may scrounge a ticket tonight and go alone."

"Oh my gosh! So weird! I signed a brand-new client this week, and he is in New York by himself too. He JUST told me he is going to see *Waitress* tonight. You would love him. Big six-foot-two Black guy with dreadlocks and a heart of solid gold. Should I connect you?"

I'm thinking: single guy, my age, alone in New York, going to see musical theater tonight . . . obviously gay. Fantastic. I could never exceed an adequate quota of gay male friends.

"Sure. Give him my number and maybe we can meet for drinks beforehand."

Ten minutes later, a ticket for *Waitress* shows up in my phone with a text: Hey this is Tyler, Heather's client. Just sent you a ticket for 7:00. We decide to meet at the Renaissance for drinks before the show.

I'm there a few minutes early and text Heather:

Thanks for connecting us! Tyler is gay, right?

Oh no. Definitely not gay. You'll see.

And as soon as I order a glass of Sancerre with fries and honey mustard, I look up and in walks a new beginning.

Chase Wonder

Listen to me: We do recover. Just keep going. Keep doing the work. Keep choosing your own freedom. Even better, we do more than recover. We *thrive*. We get to really, really live. Chase wonder and you will catch it by the tail no matter how much you have suffered. The magic has not run out.

Women are the eighth wonders of the world. May we love this little life with exposed beating hearts, tender regardless, despite it all.

Awake

It's 2:30 a.m. I'm awake.

I'm familiar with this nocturnal rhythm. I've spent a few hundred hours awake at this exact time the last two years. For a while, those middle-of-the-night hours were tempestuous, my overstimulated system triggered and hurting, anxious and urgent. The impetus always some version of this memory: "Two thirty a.m. in this bed is when it happened . . ." and then sleep was another two hours away at best.

But now I notice my body often has something gentle to communicate when the frenzy of the day finally recedes enough to tell me a few things. She'll tell me what she needs to tell me, and if I don't stay still long enough in the light of day to listen, she'll find me in the dark of night.

I lay there quietly, trusting the goodness of my own safe body, believing her wisdom and waiting for her message:

"It's two thirty."

"Yes."

"This was the time."

"Yes."

"You heard those awful words."

"Yes."

"I have a message for you too."

"What is it?"

"I just can't quit you."

I smile. My body is both cheeky and earnest. The one who will never quit me is me. The one who will never lie to me is me. The one who will always love me is me. The one who will always protect me is me. The one who will always choose me is me.

I will never again outsource my life.

When my body tells me what is true, I will believe her the first time. When she tells me what to do, I'll listen. When she tells me something is wrong, I'll trust her. When she says "This isn't good enough for you," I'll stop clinging to it. When she says "Full steam ahead," I'll move forward in joy.

I will never quit me again, which means other people will be free just to love me. Not heal, complete, validate me—that is too much pressure and not their job. That is being led around blindfolded hoping no one runs me into a wall again. My eyes are open, I can see for myself, I'm awake.

Wide awake.

Eyes bright and alive and scanning the horizon with great hope for the second half of my life.

Awake at last.

Acknowledgments

Somehow this book about a sad divorce is a love letter to the people that mean the most to me on earth. I write this section through tears. The following names represent an embarrassment of riches. I don't deserve them.

This book is the product of a brand-new crew in publishing. This is my fifteenth or sixteenth book, and my experience from start to finish has been so wildly different, I will never get over it. As a writer, I've found my home at last.

So the first thank-you goes to my new literary agent, Margaret Riley King, who pursued me for *seven years*. You displayed my books on the all-star shelf in your office where every other book was written by one of your authors . . . plus mine. You believed in me so long ago. As I prepared to write the first word of this book, you said: "Jen, save nothing for the swim home." Thank you for pushing me to the middle of the ocean. No one has ever let me go that far. I just love you.

When Margaret and I took meetings with ten different publishers at Hotel Chelsea on West Twenty-Third, an absurd rotation of literary giants, I knew quietly in my heart that Avid Reader with Simon & Schuster was my new home. I was right.

Lauren Wein, editor extraordinaire, when you handed me a *printed-out stapled booklet* of all the texts, direct messages, comments, and emails you've sent to me or written about me in the last five years, I knew we were destined. This book is just better because of you, period. Your elegant restraint to my hyperbole meant that readers did not have to endure nineteen iterations of *million, billion, trillion,* and *jillion* because exaggeration is my medium. Also thank you for flagging around one million mixed metaphors. (You can't edit my acknowledgments.) You are a master.

To the Avid team: Jofie Ferrari-Adler, Ben Loehnen, Meredith Vilarello, Amy Guay, Alison Forner, Alexandra Primiani, Caroline McGregor, Kayla Dee, Katya Wiegmann, Jessica Chin, and Eva Kerins, thank you for your embarrassing enthusiasm. It is hard to explain what it has meant to have a publishing team uninterested in bridling my words but instead raise a bullhorn in the streets on my behalf. I have felt like "a problem" for so long. To have a team of brilliant minds believe in me with no reservations has changed me not just as a writer, but as a person. *Thank you* isn't enough.

Not one thing I have written, created, produced, released, or dreamed up in the last seven years exists without my business partners, the Chandy Group. Not one. Can you even believe all this from where we started? Our stories are endless and unpublishable. You are family: Amy Chandy, Anna Trent, Pepper Sweeney, Rachel Watkins, Tosha Harrell, Jami Belew, and Ray and Amanda Garcia. We are building the world we want together. I love you. I love you. I love you. I will sing karaoke with you at Bar Marley at 2:00 a.m. while Chandy bartends *forever.*

Ten years ago, I "interviewed" (very loose term) a girl who once worked for my dad because my life had outpaced my capacity, and I needed help. I told her I had "maybe six hours of work a week" for her. A decade later, Amanda Duckett is my full-time assistant, and we are the two members of our health insurance and retirement policies. AKD, literally no one on earth knows me like you. For every Google alert you set, blackout date you guard, self-watering plant you send, and general way you make my life even possible, I can't imagine one day without you.

Moving to my friends. These pages tell the story of you, as you well know. Words actually fail me trying to say thank you, trying to say how much I love you. You held me together. You loved me back to life. You are the sisters of my heart: Jenny, Shonna, Megan, Trina, Amy, Laura, Shauna, Sarah B., Kristen, Jamie, Tara, Sarah G., the absolute best in class. I will never get over a single one of you. God, how *indulgent* that you are all mine.

As well-documented here, my OG family is the reason for every good thing in my life. How can you quantify growing up cherished and secure? What price can you put on unfailing parents and siblings who go to the ends of the earth for each other? Mom and Dad, Lindsay (+ Evan), Cortney (+ Zac), and Drew (+ Sarah), there is just no life at all without you. You rowed my boat to shore. I have never felt alone one day since I was born. I love you, family.

To Tyler, my new beginning. I found you not a day too early, not a day too late. Your easy, uncomplicated, joyful love is what I've always dreamed of. You are safe and good and true, and we are as tender as we are absurd. Thank you for loving me in stunning ways. You make me so happy. I love you, and I like you, and you are my favorite person.

Finally to my kids: Gavin (+ Danielle), Sydney, Caleb, Ben, and Remy. Guys, *you are my crew.* We hung in and hung on together, and I am so proud of who you are, who you are becoming. You are phenomenal young adults. I think you are smart and funny, interesting and creative, resilient and good. *I like you so much.* You lived a story I didn't want for you, and I got to see what you were made of. You are more than I ever hoped for, beloveds. I am your biggest fan forever.

About the Author

JEN HATMAKER is an author, podcaster, speaker, advocate, educator, mother, and a textbook Enneagram Three. From the power of her written word across fourteen books—including four *New York Times* bestsellers—to speaking on stages, leading her own courses and book club communities, and interviewing countless visionaries on her award-winning *For the Love* podcast, Jen has an undeniable gift for reaching the hearts and minds of her community.

ARP credit tk